A Chimpanzee
in the
Wine Cellar

A Chimpanzee
in the
Wine Cellar

Pat Cavendish O'Neill

JONATHAN BALL PUBLISHERS
Johannesburg & Cape Town

Pat Cavendish O'Neill is the subject of a documentary film *Toto ya Simba –
Child of the Lion: The incredible lives of Mrs O'Neill in Africa.*
Directed by Carmen Nelstein of Flynder Films, to be released in 2013.

© Pat Cavendish O'Neill, 2012
© Photographs – Unless otherwise credited all photographs used in
this book are from the author's personal collection. In the event of
any copyright infringement or error kindly contact the publisher for
it to be remedied in the event of a reprint.

First edition published in trade paperback in 2012 by
JONATHAN BALL PUBLISHERS
A division of Media24 Limited
PO Box 33977
Jeppestown
2043

Paperbook ISBN 978-1-86842-4856
eBook ISBN 978-1-86842-4870

Cover design by Michiel Botha, Cape Town
Design and typesetting by Triple M Design, Johannesburg
Printed and bound by CTP Books, Cape Town
Typeset in 11/16 pt Sabon LT Std

Twitter: www.twitter.com/JonathanBallPub
Facebook: www.facebook.com/pages/Jonathan-Ball-Publishers/
298034457992
Blog: http://jonathanball.bookslive.co.za/

I would like to dedicate this book to some very special friends without whose wonderful help and generosity I would not be living at Broadlands today surrounded by my beloved animals. To the memory of Graham Beck and to that wonderful young man Antony Beck and his mother Rhona; to Chris Myburgher, Sheila Southey and John Kalmanson, you are in my prayers every night. To my wonderful staff, with their loving support, and last but not least to Checkers Somerset West, whose past-sell-by-date food keeps my dogs, monkeys, goats, pigs and cattle well fed!

EARLY DAYS

CHAPTER

1

I have had the most incredible life, thanks to the most wonderful mother in the world, two incredible brothers and a glorious lioness called Tana who came to me as a newborn cub with her eyes still closed. Her mother had been shot down in the Tana River District and as I was well known as a compulsive rescuer of lost and injured animals I was presented with this tiny orphaned cub the moment I touched down in Nairobi to visit my younger brother Caryll. I was living in France at this time, but Tana changed all that very quickly and Kenya became my home.

My beloved and most understanding mother then bought me

a farm, called Ol Orion. It was a beautiful old colonial rambling bungalow with a magnificent garden and incredible views, and it was here that I felt I had found my place in the world. The farm bordered onto the Ngong Hills and nature reserve overlooking the Rift Valley. The area was called Karen after Karen Blixen, who wrote the book *Out Of Africa*. This period of my life will forever remain the most treasured one and the memory of my lioness Tana the most valued.

Tana was brought up on my bed, with her bottles, amidst all my dogs. I house-trained her the same way as the dogs, with her nose being rubbed into whatever mess she made inside, followed by a firm smack. She became totally house trained and over the next seven years slept on my bed alongside all the dogs and Joseph my beloved chimp, her head on the pillow beside mine, breathing short lion puffs into my ear. Tana was on my bed so often that my first book ended up being called *A Lion in the Bedroom*. The book was a bestseller in three countries and movie rights were optioned by a German company who came out to the farm one day for lunch and told me they were going to go ahead with the film. They gave me a contract to sign, which I did – stupidly, as this handed over lifetime rights to the film, and to this day they have never made it, despite the fact that the renowned British actor Dominic West was originally standing by to play the role of my lover, Stan Lawrence Brown. The book ends when I left Kenya to live in South Africa, which is where this book more or less begins.

My life in South Africa has been very different. Apart from the many tragedies, there have also been so many magical moments. In Kenya, my life was saved twice by my lioness Tana and in South Africa once again my life was saved by wild animals, this time by my baboons. I will always live in eternal gratitude for these animals and the love they have shown me.

CHAPTER

2

I was born in England, in 1925. My father was General Frederick Cavendish and at the time he was Commanding General at Aldershot in Hampshire and a highly decorated cavalry officer. He was also a 10-goal polo player and he lived his life upon a horse. I quickly followed in his footsteps and could ride before I could walk. I rode my first steeplechase at the age of six, on one of his hunters. My legs were too short and my feet too small for stirrups, so he used to slip my feet into the leather straps above the stirrups and send me on my way.

His elder brother, Harry Cavendish, inherited the family title of

Lord Waterpark, one of the Devonshire titles. As Uncle Harry had no children of his own, the title has now passed on to my brother Caryll. Our uncle was a famous explorer; he went across America with Buffalo Bill and later came through Africa. Cavendish Square, the shopping mall in Cape Town, was named after him.

My mother Enid was Australian, from the famous Lindeman Wine family. Her grandfather had come from England and bought part of the Hunter Valley, where he planted the first vineyards in Australia. My mother at one time was the sole owner of Lindeman Wines.

My mother's first husband was an American called Roderick Cameron, whose family originally came from Scotland and settled in the United States. They had clipper ships that traded with Australia and it was on one of these visits that Roderick Cameron met and fell in love with the beautiful Lindeman daughter and wanted to marry her. He was in his late thirties at the time and my grandmother, disapproving of the age difference as my mother was only 19, made him wait till she was 21.

They married in Australia in 1913 and after this Roderick took his bride to New York. They owned the Cameron Building at 185 Madison Avenue. My mother soon became a famous beauty and people used to queue to watch her arrivals and departures. In November of that same year she had a son whom she named Roderick William Cameron, known to us all as Rory, and who was later to become world famous for his infinity swimming pool design amongst other things.

Roderick Cameron died of cancer at the age of 43, leaving his young widow Enid and nine-month-old son. By this time World War I had broken out and my mother, who was never one to shy away from danger, went to France. There she bought and equipped an ambulance, which she drove herself in the frontlines.

During this time she and Rory stayed at the British Embassy in Paris. Lord Derby was the Ambassador and one of his aides threatened to commit suicide if my mother did not marry him. Lord Derby, trying to prevent the havoc my beautiful mother was creating, decided to introduce her to a famous young cavalry officer who was a colonel at the time – this was Frederick Cavendish. Soon after meeting they were married and when the war ended in 1918 he was sent to Egypt as commander of his regiment. Here my mother's beauty once again caused an uproar amongst the officers. In the 1920s and 1930s she was considered one of the six most beautiful women in the world.

After Egypt, followed by a spell in Aldershot, my father was sent to Paris as a liaison officer, as he spoke French fluently. Unlike my mother, my father was not wealthy and so it was my mother who bought the flat in Paris and the house at Le Touquet on the coast in northern France. The house was called The Berries, and there was a lovely garden and surrounding forests in which I regularly went riding. Our next-door neighbour was the famous PG Wodehouse! In addition to her great beauty, Mummy rode beautifully, played golf, drove a car, which in those days was unusual for a woman, and she was also a very good artist and musician. She was quite simply the most incredible and loving mother one could wish for!

We were with my mother holidaying at Biarritz in southwest France when she got news of my father's death. His valet had found him dead of a cerebral haemorrhage on the floor of their Paris apartment. I was six years old at the time.

My mother's next husband was Viscount Furness, owner of a shipping empire and one of the world's richest men. He fell instantly in love when he saw her enter the casino at Le Touquet. He vowed to his friends at the time that this was the lady he was going to marry as he had never seen such perfection before. He then pursued her relentlessly. My mother had a flat in Chester Square in London and so he bought the whole building and gave her the deeds made out in her name.

Furness refused to use public transport. He also refused to let my mother travel anywhere on public transport. He had his own private plane and pilot standing by, as well as a private train with his own station and two ocean-going liners, the *Emerald* and the *Sapphire*, with a crew of 40 per vessel. His dogged determination to win my mother over eventually succeeded.

After their wedding in 1933, they went to live in his huge Victorian mansion, Burrough Court, in Leicestershire. Furness had a staff of over 100 people which included four cooks, a butler, six footmen in full livery, a boot boy just to clean shoes and a host of groundsmen, grooms and cleaning staff. My brother Caryll and I had one whole wing of the building, with our own staff and a chauffeur. I never went to school and arithmetic was not on my schedule – I could hardly add and subtract, thank goodness now for calculators, not known in my day – but I had a tutor, two governesses and my beloved nanny, who remained with me until I was 18, as I was never allowed out by myself. It was only after I turned 18 and Nanny Peabody retired that I was allowed to go out unaccompanied, much to my eventual delight! Despite this rigid chaperoning, from an early age I spent my days on a horse and driving cars around the estate. My younger brother was flying and landing my stepfather's aeroplanes at the age of 11. My mother never knew the meaning of fear, so this was how Caryll and I were brought up.

My mother kept all my father's retainers. Frederick's cavalry sergeant-major gave me military training and every morning in the large covered arena I would be drilled over the jumps with arms crossed and the reins knotted on the horse's neck. 'Go with the horse!' he would shout as he waved his riding crop in the air.

We used to go hunting with the Cottesmore and the Quorn Hunts twice a week and on the other days we would ride all over my step-father's vast estate.

Furness had magnificent stables for all his riding horses and hunters. He was fanatical about cleanliness so the stables had to be spotless. The entrance to each stable was white-chalked and the straw plaited by the doors. The tack room had an enormous number of silver cups and plates on display in glass cabinets. Each saddle and blanket for over 80 horses had its own rack with a bridle polished to perfection hanging overhead. There were two boys employed full-time just to clean the tack every day and iron the saddle-cloths. Furness also owned two famous stud farms, Gilltown in Ireland, which upon his death was bought by Aga Khan III, and Sandley House in Dorset, which became the first National Stud in England. Many famous racehorses, including Nearco, were bred there. Mummy and Furness were great racing enthusiasts, so I got to know all these wonderful studs and horses.

My mother had kept my father's army blacksmith, who now took over the stable forge at Burrough Court. He and his assistant did all the shoeing. I used to spend a lot of my free time helping him whenever he let me. I would listen quietly while he told me tales of my father's bravery and proudly showed me a very battered book written about my father. I never worried about the fact that I had no other children to play with. My brother Caryll had gone off to Hawtreys and then on to Eton and only came back for holidays. My older brother Rory now lived in London in a flat Mummy had bought for him.

We were not allowed into the front of the house, except in the mornings, when we used to go to our mother's room, where she would be surrounded by her dogs and two tame silver foxes. It was the highlight of my day, the two hours I spent with our mother each morning as well as when she used to visit me every night. Furness hated children; even his own did not meet with his approval. His daughter Averill, who was from his first marriage, married Andrew Rattray, who was a white hunter – this in Furness's mind was an inferior occupation so he promptly disinherited her. Andrew was the uncle of South Africa's famous Mike Rattray, owner of game reserves, racehorses and a magnificent stud.

I adored Averill's younger brother, Christopher, who was known to us as Dick Furness. He was my hero. He did not come to Burrough Court that often, though he kept some of his steeple-chasers there and trusted me enough to let me school them for him. Furness wanted to disinherit him as well because he gave a drunken party at Burrough Court at which he and his friends fished all the exotic collection of fish out of the massive tropical fish tank that made up one of the walls of the billiard room. My mother also loved Dick and threatened to leave Furness if he did disinherit him. Furness relented but Dick was never allowed back to Burrough Court. In 1940, during World War II, he was killed at the battle of Dunkirk. He made a famous cavalry charge in his tank to draw the enemy fire away from his troops and was awarded England's high-est military honour, the Victoria Cross.

Furness refused to recognise his other son by his second wife, Thelma. He always claimed that this son, William, was the bastard son of the Prince of Wales, later King Edward VIII, with whom Thelma had been having an affair. Thelma introduced the Prince to her great friend Wallis Simpson, for whom he then deserted Thelma and later gave up the throne of England.

After having been humiliated by his second wife, Furness was obsessed with discouraging any would-be future husbands from getting near his lovely wife – my mother. He bought her a famous house called La Fiorentina in the South of France, on the point of St

Jean Cap Ferrat. Because he was so jealous of his beautiful wife, he gradually bought up all the other houses on the point, which overlooked the Bay of Beaulieu and Monte Carlo. This was to ensure that no lovers could move in nearby.

In France my mother's famous looks continued to bring things to a standstill. Once, when accompanied by Furness on a first visit to the casino at Monte Carlo, the news got around that they had arrived and as my mother entered, gambling came to a stop. Tables were deserted as my mother appeared in a Molyneux gown, wearing the famous Furness diamonds and tiara. King Farouk of Egypt said to her, 'Enid, darling, next time please come with a yashmak and burka, as your beautiful presence has ruined my game!'

When they had been married seven years, Furness fell very ill and had to have two night nurses and two day nurses. It was 1940 and the last refugee ship was waiting to take the English out of France before the Germans arrived. Somerset Maugham, who was a neighbour, came to see Mummy and tried to persuade her that despite Furness's ill-health we would have to risk the journey. Anyone left behind would certainly end up in a concentration camp, he said. When my mother finally got Furness to Cannes where the ship was moored, he took one look at the vessel, referred to it as a fucking tramp steamer and refused to go on board! He said to Mummy, 'You can take your fucking daughter, but I am not going.'

We spent that night at the Carlton Hotel in Cannes. Mummy told me to go to my room, then came later to tell me that she had arranged for me to leave with Willie Maugham, as Furness was too ill and she could not leave him. Naturally I flatly refused to go, so we all returned to La Fiorentina. My stepfather died soon after this. Mummy and I were in the basement, where the huge kitchen was, melting down candles to make soap, when the nurse came to call her. She left me in charge of all the huge pots, telling me not to let them boil over. In those days there were no televisions so one used to read books. I had a vivid imagination and in the dimly lit kitchen I imagined all these devils peering out at me from behind the boiling cauldrons. It was a nightmare which even to this day I remember so clearly.

The South of France became part of Vichy France and there was a big prisoner of war camp at Aize. After Furness's death, Mummy started rescuing English prisoners; she even rescued a famous American, Whitney Straight, who had joined the Royal Air Force. On one occasion, she dressed them up as maids and had them on their knees polishing the floors by the time the Germans arrived. There was, I believe, an escape route somewhere in Nice that she used to send them to.

On another occasion, my mother got me to ride on a bicycle with her lady's maid, Mlle Jeanne, and an English prisoner whom she dressed as one of the gardeners, complete with beret, to get him safely from Cap Ferrat to Nice. She thought that we would just look like a poor family group and therefore not raise any suspicions. At that age, not having been taught the meaning of fear, passing the Germans on motorbikes meant nothing to me. So we delivered him safely.

Despite my mother's best efforts, things got gradually worse and worse and we were soon forced to leave. The Germans were getting very suspicious and how we got across the frontier on the escape route I do not know. My mother had rolled up my long hair to make curls on top of my head into which she pinned bank notes, but I don't remember another thing until we were on a terrible train going across Spain and the toilette was full of old women sitting on the floor with their trussed chickens. I remember the agony of not being able to go to the loo; I was much too shy to go in front of anybody. We finally arrived at the British Embassy in Portugal.

There, my mother used her influence to get us on the regular flying-boat service to England. I remember the trip clearly, as in order to avoid anti-aircraft guns, we had to fly just above sea level and the beautiful moon was shining on the water.

We arrived back in London just in time for the Battle of Britain. Furness's London home, Lees Place, was just off Grosvenor Square and was a very lovely eighteenth-century building, set back in a semi-courtyard with its own stables and a little lane to the right leading towards Hyde Park. The stables now functioned as garages for the Rolls-Royces, the only cars Furness would have.

So that we would not worry about all the bombing, Mummy would take us up to the top balcony as soon as the sirens rang and would give pocket money to whoever could count the most bombs coming out of the bays. As a result Caryll and I could not wait for the sirens to go off and we would race each other up to the balcony to see who could get there first. Once, as we stood on the balcony, a huge bomb came sailing right past us: I ducked as it flew by and landed in one of our garages. It never went off and the whole of Grosvenor Square was evacuated as the bomb had to be disassembled. My mother refused to go, saying, 'Our boys are risking their lives for us, we will not desert them.' So we stayed and I watched the whole process. One soldier actually mounted the huge bomb and it was so large that even his legs did not touch the floor.

Shortly after this Caryll was sent to Sandhurst where he became a military cadet and won the belt of honour – and I was sent to a secretarial school to learn shorthand and typing. As Rory had been born in the United States he held American citizenship and so during the war he was a sergeant in the American intelligence. He had been educated in America, Switzerland and Germany, so he was fluent in German and French. He was later sent to London, on loan to British intelligence, where he worked with Hugh Trevor-Roper and helped with the research on his famous book, *The Last Days of Hitler*. In fact, according to Rory, he actually wrote most of it as well.

Mummy was a great friend of General Eisenhower and the American Ambassador at the time, so I ended up working at the American Embassy. I was luckily allowed to take my dogs to work with me. It was an easy morning walk across the square, with all its grass and lovely trees. There was hardly any traffic, as there was almost no petrol available, and during the tea breaks or if the sirens went off, instead of going down to the bomb shelter I would go and sit in the park with the dogs.

Mummy and I used to go to Battersea Lost Dogs Home on rescue missions and then the dogs would be driven down to our house in Wales for Lane, one of Mummy's lady's maids, to look after. By this time Lane must have had 40 or 50 dogs in her keeping. So many of them had been rescued from bombed-out buildings in which their owners had been killed. It was a tradition my mother started of saving dogs – in fact she could never resist rushing to the assistance and rescue of any animal in pain – which to this day I have continued.

Because I could do shorthand in both French and Spanish, I rose in a fairly short time from lowly filing clerk to having an office of my own. I think I was the youngest member of staff to be in that position. After the war I was asked if I would go to Paris and work for the Americans at Orly. Here I ended up having to work on some of the court martials. I used to feel so sorry for the culprits. I stayed in Paris with my Aunt Mimi, who had been married to my uncle, Harry Waterpark. Talk about sexual harassment, from generals to GIs. I had to have a special corset made like a chastity belt!

During the war Mummy had met up with one of her ex-admirers. I adored him; he was Viscount Castlerosse, Earl of Kenmare, better known as Valentine Castlerosse. He wrote a column for the Beaverbrook Press and had also written a life of Tolstoy and *The Young Mr Pitt*, which a very famous film was made of. I was so pleased when they married as he was a *bon viveur* in every sense. After marrying him Mummy took the title of Countess of Kenmare.

Valentine was tall but very portly as he kept stuffing himself with food and drink. On top of this he was a heavy gambler and had gone through most of his inheritance by the time Mummy came along. He had a bad heart and had been told to cut down on his eating and drinking habits and take some exercise. He paid no attention to Mummy's strictures, even though food was in very short supply! But she did get him to accompany me to the park each day to walk the dogs when I got back from the Embassy. He was so fascinating and with my love of history he kept me enthralled for hours.

Despite the fact that it was war time, we managed to go on some wonderful holidays to Ireland. Valentine's vast estate was there, right on the Killarney lakes, and with my mother's money a beautiful golf course around the lakes was designed by Henry Cotton. Both my mother and Valentine were keen golfers, which was how they had met at Le Touquet years before. Today I believe Kenmare House is a hotel.

Mummy, I and Rory were at Lees Place when the terrible news of Valentine's death in Ireland came through. He had died of a heart attack. Mummy left the next day for Ireland. Although she had so many suitors, including Prince Pierre de Polignac, the father of Prince Rainier of Monaco, Mummy said that marrying her seemed to be unlucky, and she was never going to marry again. From then on, my beloved brother Rory took over. Although my adored mother was multi-talented, she had always depended on the man in her life. When we came to South Africa many years later, I took over and she used to laugh and complain that it was like living with a governess.

Following my stint at Orly Airport, I went to the United States, as my aunt – or rather Rory's aunt, the formidable Mrs Cameron Tiffany – wanted me to spend a year with her. She had hated me as a 14-year-old child when we had driven across America with her. But by now things had changed. Her son, George Tiffany, had been a colonel in the American Air Force and was a bomber pilot. When he came to London, he always came to visit and used to ask me to go out with him to dinners and the theatre. I was immensely shy at the time, as I had never been allowed out on the streets by myself until I was 18. In fact, my first encounter as an 18-year-old with a 'would-be' boyfriend was with a GI in Hyde Park. He used to meet me there when I was walking the dogs. One day we were sitting on a bench together and he kissed me, my first kiss, but then he put his tongue in my mouth and I promptly fainted. An alarming occurrence for him, but one that was quite normal for me, as I was always fainting in my youth, passing out with a loud moan, much to everyone's embarrassment.

Rumours used to circulate in London that I was retarded and this was entirely due to my shyness. Once when some friends, the Sitwells, came to visit, I was in the entrance hall when the butler let them in, and had no chance to escape. I was wearing a red dress at the time and they saw my backside disappearing under the tapestry cover that was decorating the hall table. When they asked the butler who I was, he said 'That's Miss Pat, her Ladyship's daughter, but she is very shy.' I think they thought he was finding a polite way of saying I was retarded.

Another of my dreadfully embarrassing fainting fits came in Paris. I loved skating and there was a charity gala event at which the Prince of Wales was guest of honour. It was all very grand and the rink was packed with socialites. Our friend, Princess Elizabeth Chavchavadze, was taking the part of Catherine the Great of Russia and being pulled along in her carriage by skaters dressed up as horses, and then we came at the rear, myself and a friend, Jimmy Douglas, a very good-looking young American whose father was a VIP in the American government. While we had practised all the waltzes, the outfits designed by Dior had only arrived the morning of the gala; mine was a huge velvet skirt, with a tight hussar-like top. After the waltz and the end of our act, we all turned and the men bowed and the ladies curtseyed to the Prince of Wales in the royal box. As I sank in my curtsey and tried to get up, the serrated edge of my skates caught in my skirt, pulling me down again, and in the struggle I broke my thumb. There I was, flopping about on the ice like a plucked chicken. Jimmy pulled me up by grabbing my hand with the broken thumb; I just made it to the exit, where once again I passed out. I was told that when they took my glove off, the thumb fell back against my wrist. When I went up to Mummy's box, she was practically in tears: 'I am told you were drunk and passed out on the ice,' she wailed. I don't think she entirely believed me about the broken thumb, until I had to go the following morning to get X-rays and a plaster cast.

Needless to say, after my very first fainting episode with the GI in the park, it was the last I saw of him. I remember going home to Lees Place and looking at myself in the mirror and wondering if I was pregnant. I then asked my mother's lovely lady's maid, Maureen, who very kindly took the trouble to explain the facts of life.

So one night after dinner, when George Tiffany, Aunt Cameron Tiffany's son, asked me back to Claridges, a luxurious hotel in Mayfair where he was staying, I unsuspectingly accompanied him. There was a bottle of champagne on ice, but Mummy did not approve of women drinking, so I just had a couple of sips, before he started kissing me. I had been very strictly brought up to never be anything but respectful to your elders. He seemed like an old man at the time; when you are 18 anyone in their late thirties appears old. I was desperately trying to fend him off without being rude, when next thing he was on top of me, trying to get my pants off, so once again I passed out. I think he got the fright of his life; he had kept telling me how in love he was with me and how he wanted to marry me. He did take me out a few times after that and I was terrified that Mummy would agree to his proposal of marriage. Sadly for his mother, he was killed on one of his bombing missions, but in his last letter home he had told her that he loved me and wanted to marry me and what a wonderful girl I was. This was why she now wanted me to go and spend a year with her in the United States.

I must say, as formidable as she was, Aunt Nanny was wonderful to me. She had a lovely house in Charleston, South Carolina, right on the sea, another beautiful house in Boston, and her flat in New York took up the entire top floor of the Cameron Building. I loved America; she took me everywhere and the Americans were so friendly and warm-hearted to me. This was in such contrast to France where I was used to being so much younger than our guests that often days could go by without any of them speaking to me. Also, I do not think they thought I was at all *comme il faut*.

CHAPTER

3

My trip with Aunt Nanny ended at Mummy's house on Cable Beach in the Bahamas, where she knew everyone, so we were continually entertaining or being entertained. Being with Aunt Nanny, the formalities had to be observed and she insisted we write our names down at Government House. While I stood musing over the love of the Duke of Windsor – the previous Governor – for Wallis Simpson, and picturing them in the room where we now stood, I looked up and saw the most beautiful, elegant young man walking by, his arms full of papers. He was very tall and had all the dark brooding beauty of a Byronic character. He was so perfect for this exotic setting that for a moment I thought he was part of my imagination.

The new hero of my dreams was Richard Murphy, the son of the Governor. Within weeks we were engaged to be married. There was a very grand engagement party and when everyone stood up to give the royal toast, I suddenly felt my fainting fit about to appear. I panicked, made some excuse and fled towards the nearest ladies' room. One had to go through the entrance hall, where there were a lot of columns. I started to pass out before getting there and the last thing I remember before everything went black was grabbing one of the columns as I sank to the floor and a lady's voice in the distance, saying, 'She is obviously drunk.'

As the wedding drew near, I got in a panic and wrote a letter calling it off. My mother was not at all pleased with her headstrong daughter and decided it was time to visit her beloved family in Australia. Every year either they came to France or she and I would visit them. It was on this voyage that I met the next love of my life, my beloved husband Frank, who I married and divorced – and married again, much later, which gives me an excuse to tell his story in a later chapter.

* * *

Single once again, I joined my mother and Rory in Paris. Rory's new girlfriend, Princess Elizabeth Chavchavadze, lived on the Rue Hamelin and Mummy had rented the top floor, which Rory had turned into a large apartment.

One night as we came down for dinner, the first person I saw as we entered the sitting room was the tall, beautifully elegant figure of Guy de Lesseps, standing by the fireplace talking to one of the guests. I was 16 the last time I had seen him, in a theatre in Cannes during the war, and he was the first man I had ever fallen in love with. He had the head and body of a classical Greek statue, with his close-cropped dark blond curly hair, aquiline nose, beautiful sexy mouth and slumberous amber eyes – I was utterly smitten! Then, as if he knew I had entered the room, he looked up. I could feel my heart dive and accelerate, as leaving the very chic woman he had been talking to he came across the room to me. He was very tall and as he bent over my hand to kiss it, he looked at me with amused eyes, '*Ma belle Patricia, pourquoi tu m'as fait attendre si longtemps?*'

I could feel myself blushing; knowing women so well he was amused at my reaction to him. He spent the rest of the evening with me, flirting outrageously and enjoying my acute embarrassment at his excessive compliments. Afterwards he told me that it was such a refreshing change from women who expected flattery as their due. I was of course a lot younger than the women he was used to. He was 39 at the time and I was now 26. He had been living with the artist Nora Auric since he was 23 and she was 20 years older than him. In today's world he would have been known as a 'toy boy', but that nomenclature was unknown in those days. He was famous just for being the beautiful young lover of Nora Auric, wife of the famous French composer, Georges Auric!

The fact that Comte Guy de Lesseps was the grandson of the famous Ferdinand de Lesseps, who built the Suez Canal, seemed of no importance to French society. But I found this hugely significant and had wonderful, romantic memories of the Suez Canal and his grandfather's life-size statue decorating the banks of this incredible waterway – the gateway to Africa. Since the age of 10, memories of the Canal, the romance of Africa, the mystery, the beauty of this wonderful continent have entranced me. It was as if I had been brought so deep into its embrace that it was never to let me go.

This of course made Guy even more attractive and alluring. His voice was so beautiful, he was fluent in both English and French, and here he was telling me that I was *une beauté* and that he had never forgotten me since that memorable evening on the staircase. I could not believe, with all the beautiful, intelligent and sophisticated women he had met, that a young girl of 16 climbing the steps to the theatre during wartime could have remained in his memory.

At one stage Nora came over and said, 'I see Guy is embarrassing you with all his attention, don't worry, he is passionate about women and you are a *nouveauté*.' Before I left he asked me to meet him at a bistro on the Champs Elysées. I went home on cloud nine and all I could think of was that I would be meeting Guy again and that he must find me attractive, or he would not bother to make a date. From then on, week after week I used to meet him every day, sometimes for two or three hours, or sometimes for 15 minutes between his engagements. I knew he loved being with me, but in all that time he never tried to carry our relationship beyond his outrageous flirting.

One strange thing was that Nora, as long as he was with me, did not seem to mind. I did not know what Guy had told her, but she realised we had a lot in common and since cars and horses bored her and I was not at all sophisticated and was often with my family as chaperones, she probably judged that not too much could take place.

Guy was a very good rally driver and loved cars and so did I. He also loved riding and horses, and we both loved dancing. I think he had persuaded Nora that I was much too young and was only interested in the same sports as him.

It was on one of these nights while we sat chatting in a bistro in

Les Halles, when Nora was at a concert, that I looked up and saw two magnificent Percherons passing by. They had to stop near the red light just outside where we were sitting. Because of Furness and his famous Percheron stud, I was thrilled to see these beautiful horses, so I rushed out to talk to them and to their owner. To my horror I learned that they were on their way to the abattoir. There and then I paid the owner double what the butcher would have paid, leaving Guy to bargain with the owner who was refusing at this point to take them back to the stable. I stood in the Parisian traffic holding these two huge horses for what seemed like hours while Guy plied their owner with wine and more money to get him to agree to take them home for the night. Mummy had a lovely house with a garden at 37 Rue de l'Université but there was not enough room for two huge carthorses.

I did not know anyone in France with a farm nearby who would take two carthorses, so Guy spent the rest of the night calling up friends, and eventually he found some with a farm not far from Paris. They must have been amazed to be awoken in the early hours of the morning to have two Percherons thrust upon them.

The story soon got around; Nora was highly amused, and was now convinced I was a total screwball who would hold no real interest for the very sophisticated Guy de Lesseps. Her one stricture was: 'If you are going out in the evening with him do not let him drink too much, he is far too fond of his wine.' She never said anything about rescuing horses!

We then left for the South of France. A few weeks later Guy and Nora went to their house at Porquerolles. As Georges Auric, Nora's husband, was not there, Guy spent most of his time with Nora. They quite often came over for lunch and whenever he had free time, he would call up and I would drive over with my dogs and meet him on the beach. Even in those days, without much traffic, it was a fairly long drive over narrow winding roads. Often he would only have time for a quick swim and few minutes of conversation sitting under the beach umbrella that I used to carry in the boot of the car. I was so besotted with him that just these few minutes were precious and the long drive home was passed in euphoric memories of his passionate looks and the feel of his beautiful tanned body as he lay beside me on the beach.

Guy and Nora then went off to Spain and I was in despair as weeks went by without my seeing him, but finally we were all meeting up in Venice. We were once again staying with Princess Chavchavadze in her palazzo on the Grand Canal and they were going to stay in a hotel. We were all meeting in the Piazza del Marco.

The sight of him walking towards us was unforgettable. As he bent over to kiss my hand, I felt almost faint with emotion. He looked up and in a whisper said those magic words: '*Ma belle Patricia, que je t'aime.*' He then drew up a chair and sat down beside me; in the general conversation no more was said. He almost ignored me but under the table his leg touched mine. I tried to give him space, but he wouldn't have it.

When, finally, we did make love it was in his flat in Montmartre. The experience was so incredible that, unsurprisingly, on the way to the bathroom I passed out.

I had been raised on my mother's precepts: 'Never be afraid, never be ill – and if you are don't talk about it – and above all, never be jealous.' For Guy, however, my attitude was incomprehensible. From then on his jealousy became obsessive. The fact that I was not worried about his having lady friends and never questioned him about his love life convinced him that there was someone else in my life. He was never abusive, but it was the continual questioning and suspicion of my every movement that finally drove me to disappear back to London.

Since Mummy hated winter we followed the sun back to the Bahamas. There I met my next husband, Aymon de Roussy de Sales, more of whom in the second part of the book.

* * *

After the war Rory's restoration had made La Fiorentina one of the most famous houses in the world. He designed the first swimming pool of the type that is now known as an infinity pool. He also designed a wonderful garden and beautiful walks between the various houses. Another first for Rory was at a restaurant in Eze when he seized a doormat and much to my horror took it to the manager to find out where it had come from. The result was the first sisal carpets.

Rory also taught me photography. Years later, when *Architectural Review* was doing an article on La Fiorentina, they used all my photographs. I have framed so many of them and to this day, I look back with nostalgia at my photographs of Mummy and Rory and the beautiful villas that Mummy owned in the South of France.

I just could not live without Mummy and Rory. Even my long-suffering husbands had to come and live with my family. Around this time we also spent two wonderful years in India. I had my thirtieth birthday on my mother's houseboat, on the beautiful Dhal Lake in Kashmir. I loved the Indians and their magnificent country; they were so wonderfully hospitable to us. We stayed in fabulous palaces with famous Maharajas, where I could go riding every day, as well as in tiny bungalows with buckets for toilets – this was because Rory wanted to experience all aspects of India. The hospitality and the incredible sense of colour were unforgettable.

After his death Rory was given a Creative Capital Award for all he had done for art and architecture, which Caryll and I flew over to Washington to receive. There is now also a room at the museum in Nice in France which is dedicated to him for all he did for garden design and botany. Being so multi-talented, he was a brilliant photographer as well and his photographs of our time in India were given an exhibition in London. Mrs Gandhi attended the opening.

Seeing the world through Rory's eyes was a life of continual enchantment. Looking back, I realise how incredibly privileged I was to spend so many years travelling in his wake as he and Mummy, following the sun, did the grand tours of Italy, Greece, Egypt, Ceylon and India. We always travelled by ship to accommodate the mountain of luggage and the unbelievable collection of *objets d'art* they amassed between them.

CHAPTER

4

When my mother was married to Furness, they used to go to Kenya for four or five months every year on safari. I think this was one of Furness's ploys to get his beautiful wife away from so many adoring suitors. Furness had his own plane, with a famous pilot called Campbell Black, so he was able to fly in whatever provisions were necessary; he also had a fleet of Rolls-Royces equipped as safari cars which were a famous sight in Kenya for many years. Campbell Black had an affair with a young Kenyan woman called Beryl Markham who became the first woman to fly the Atlantic. Beryl became very famous and wrote a book about her experiences called *West with the Night*. In addition she was not only very beautiful, but also a great horsewoman, and became Kenya's top racehorse trainer. As a child, I used to see her when she came to Burrough Court with Campbell Black. Little did I know then what a dramatic impact on my life she would have in the years to come.

I was 10 when my mother took us on our first safari. My brother Caryll and I fell in love with Kenya. After the end of the war, Caryll decided that he wanted to live in Kenya, so Mummy bought him a magnificent farm up in the White Highlands, at Subukia. The Equator ran right through the farm, which inspired Rory to write a book called *Equator Farm*.

My mother and I would go and visit Caryll every year and eventually Mummy also built her own house on the farm. Caryll, being Caryll, had to have his own aeroplane, so he built himself a landing strip which made coming and going so much easier. Caryll had always been a brilliant pilot and years later when he left Kenya, he became head of CSE Aviation, which taught all the British Airways pilots and those of various other nations as well.

It was on one of these many visits to Caryll that I was presented with Tana. Tiny wee Tana who curled up in the palm of my hand and changed my life forever. Here in Kenya with my beloved Tana, I was to spend the most wonderful years of my life.

I lived in the most wonderful country in the world, as Kenya was in those days, I had my glorious farm and adored African staff, they looked after me like a child and I was surrounded by the beautiful tribes of Africa. It was indeed a dream world.

Now that I had a house of my own, I seemed somehow or other to have become a collecting point for unwanted or injured animals. It happened so gradually that I hardly realised how involved I had become. Apart from Tana, Joseph the chimpanzee, rescued from what was then the Belgian Congo, and Duma, the cheetah, I had a baboon named Jason who had been rescued from a tree in Arusha, several vervet monkeys, two Sykes' monkeys and a very rare owl-faced monkey from the Congo. A bushbuck, two baby warthogs, two genets and two crowned cranes used to wander around the garden. As well as the wild animals there were my five precious Bahamian wild dogs, Rogue, Smokey and Bandit and also the two poodles, Minou and Minette, Panya the pug and Duke the Alsatian. Afterwards I rescued an Alsatian bitch that I called Duchess. All the domestic animals were neutered, including the various cats.

There were so many dogs that my mother decided to send out Miss Lane who was still with her. She was given her own cottage on the farm and saw to all the feeding and grooming. It was lovely having her, this familiar figure from my childhood. When she had first arrived at Burrough Court as assistant lady's maid, she had been a pretty young woman with large brown eyes and curly hair. She soon graduated to looking after all my mother's wild pets and canines. I remembered her walking the lanes of Leicestershire with packs of dogs because Furness did not like them going into the fields amongst the cattle and horses. Now she was grey and rather bent. A chain-smoker, she always had a cigarette in her mouth and my mother was always telling her off for it. Lane would just laugh and cough away. In Kenya, she would insist on still helping with my mother's clothes but as Mummy said, she would much prefer she did not. She would say, 'Lane, you look like a dog, smell like a dog and have less sense. They at least don't smoke and put cigarette ash all over my clothes.'

Tana was never enclosed, even when she became a fully grown lioness, and she grew up as part of the family with Joseph and the dogs. Kenya being the relaxed place it was in those days, I could take her wherever I liked. My great friends Tubby and Aino Block owned most of the hotels and lodges in Kenya and used to regularly and happily host Tana and me. I had a special harness made for Tana and together we would walk through these public places, much to the amazement of many.

The Blocks also had a lovely house and a hotel at Nyali Beach on the coast near Mombasa. We used to have such a wonderful time down there as we could all charge around on the beautiful beaches. They used to welcome us all – a chimp, a lioness, six dogs, a rescued Thomson's gazelle called Tim Tom and often a few more rescues ... and me.

On one of our visits there, little Tim Tom, who always lay beside me on the front seat when we were driving, got a fright when a vulture hit my windscreen and leapt straight out of the car. Watching in horror, I saw him tumble over and over, and raced back convinced that he would be dead. Amazingly, he was not, though he was in shock and had broken a front leg. I had to rush him to a vet in Mombasa, where his leg was put in a cast. Thank goodness they did a marvellous job and he recovered completely, though for the first few days I had to carry him around with his leg on a pillow.

When Tana was a mature lioness, she would come in season and then we used to have continual visits from the male lions in the area. I got so used to the roaring that I hardly heard them any more, but my guests used to complain, especially when my friend Bini Malcolm came home late one night and met up with a lion on my front doorstep. Thinking the lioness was Tana, Bini went shoo with her handbag and was amazed when the lioness roared and backed away. She then opened the front door to find Tana asleep on the sofa in the sitting room. Realising she had just shooed away a wild lion, she and I then went to the door with torches and counted 23 lions that had taken up residence in the garden.

Suchil Gurham, who was a great friend at the time and a very good bridge player, often used to come and play with my mother, who was a bridge addict. Suchil told Bini that when Tana used to come and sit by the bridge table, he got so nervous that he did not dare take a trick, in case Enid got upset – and if Enid were upset, who knew what Tana would do! Suchil was president of the Oxford Union and a leading lawyer in Kenya. After Independence, he became the first non-white president of the famous Muthaiga Club.

Bini also reminded me of how fond my mother was of my great friend Margaret Kenyatta. She worried so much about her, the reason being that her adored father was in prison for being head of the Mau Mau and that she had two children and a not very happy marriage. So my mother practically adopted her. Her father was Jomo Kenyatta. When Kenya got its independence, he became prime minister and what a remarkable man he turned out to be; another great leader of his country, like the wonderful Madiba of South Africa.

The chimpanzee Joseph would spend his time with my mother as she taught him to paint on large canvases and they adored each other. It was a wonderful sight: my glorious mother, Joseph, and Tikki her hyrax, all enjoying a painting session. Mummy not only painted canvases and screens, but did all the dining room and furniture in the most wonderful grey and white marbling.

I was in my early thirties and when my mother was not there, I lived on my own. My wonderful Wakamba staff were all men; women never worked as domestics in those days. They were too busy labouring on their *shamba*s at home, carrying unbelievable loads of firewood from a thong attached to their foreheads which hung down their backs. They would walk for miles up and down the hills of Africa. The men's quarters at my house at Karen were away from the house, near the forest area.

I had a wonderful lover, Stan Lawrence Brown, one of the most famous of Kenya's elite band of white hunters. Seeing this land through his eyes showed me a country of miracles. He taught me so much. It's probably not that surprising that we fell in love. Although he had made his living out of hunting animals and I only wanted to save them, a hunter has to be almost psychic with animals: as Stan would say to me, 'You have to understand them, read them and understand their country.'

Knowing the habits of the wild, Stan tried to teach me its ways and through his knowledge I came to see Africa with different eyes. We would walk for days and miles following elephant. He always carried a gun, but it was never fired. He let me experience the excitement of the hunt without being the hunter. How marvellous to come right up under an enormous bull elephant after several days of following his trail and be able to stand silently watching him as he browsed on the trees in passing. Once we came upon a herd grazing on a field of white flowers. I sat entranced for hours as mothers with their babies walked through this dream garden, lifting great bunches of flowers in their trunks, looking like brides going to a wedding. For days I would close my eyes and recall the beauty of this scene.

There was a Kikuyu uprising at the time known as the Mau Mau. All my friends said I was crazy living on my own, so far away from everyone and with no security. I was not worried; Tana would take care of me. They would be brave people who tangled with her and my staff were not that far away. However, friends did persuade me to build a security fence from my bedroom to the sitting room, as the only telephone in the house was there. From my room to the sitting room, there was a long open veranda and it was this that I employed some workmen to cover with a security fence. The house was a very large single-storey bungalow with a shingle roof and built in an L-shape. My bedroom was at the bottom of the L overlooking a large natural forest which went down to a river, full of monkeys and wildlife. The house also had several guest cottages, as when Mummy was there so many overseas visitors came to stay. There was a tree in the courtyard, which Tana would jump onto and from there she could leap up onto the roof. Tana liked to lie on the roof under the shade of the tree. When she was not asleep she kept an eye on what was going on down below.

It is amazing how one can communicate with wild animals. One hot afternoon I was in my bathroom bathing Joseph the chimpanzee when suddenly I could pick up Tana's feeling of rage. I rushed out of the bathroom and saw Tana on the roof, about to leap onto one of the men doing my security fence. Tana, although a huge lioness by now, was the gentlest of creatures. She had never shown any signs of aggression and was very obedient, so I shouted at her to back off. I said to the headman, 'She has never tried to attack anyone before. We will forget about the security fence and I will pay you off at once.'

Ten days later, at about two in the morning, Tana leapt off my bed and started pacing up and down by the large window that overlooked the forest. I sat up in bed and watched her and could feel she was trying to tell me that I was about to be attacked. I realised that she was alerting me that the Mau Mau were coming. On the way to the telephone, I thought, I cannot call the police and tell them that the Mau Mau are coming. 'How do you know?' they will ask. 'Well, my lioness told me,' would be my reply.

I called up anyway and said, 'I think the Mau Mau have arrived on the farm.' They told me they had no transport and asked me to come and get them. I had a big three-ton International safari car that Stan had given me, so I went to the Karen police station, which was about a 20 minute drive, and loaded up with the police askaris.

33

When we arrived back about an hour later, the farm was still in darkness and there was no sign of anything happening. The askaris all disappeared into the night and I was left feeling like an idiot. About 10 minutes later, there was suddenly the sound of battle; the Mau Mau had just arrived. The gang was taken by surprise and were all arrested. Now I had to drive the prisoners back in two trips – and suddenly, as I was pulling away, I had a pair of handcuffs around my throat trying to throttle me from behind. The askari sitting next to him hit the man on his head with his truncheon and I turned to see that the leader of the gang had been the same man making my security fence. So my beloved Tana had picked up his feelings of hatred from the roof and that is why she had tried to spring on him.

But how she knew they were coming and was able to warn me, at least an hour before their arrival, is amazing and I owe my life to her. Apparently the Mau Mau gang had assembled about a mile beyond the river to plot their assault, a distance of at least three miles away from the farm, which was around the time she became so agitated.

Several years later, Tana and I were walking in the Masai Mara when she again saved my life. I was admiring the setting sun at the time and due to its angle I did not make out the darkened outline of a herd of buffalo. We were downwind from them, making the situation extremely dangerous. Tana suddenly threw me to the ground and sat on top of me. A lion is the buffalo's greatest enemy so I was as safe as could be under the weight of my beloved lioness.

It was on safari at the Tana River that my beloved little companion Tim Tom was killed. I had been running with Tana one evening on the river's edge, splashing her with water and throwing her favourite ball to her. Suddenly I got the most terrible feeling that something dreadful was happening. I told myself, 'It's the sunset making you feel this way, because it's darker than usual.' But I could not shake the feeling, so I left our game and rushed back up to the lodge, which was still mostly a tented camp. Everything looked calm, so I went to find Stan. I told him of my feelings, so he took some men to search around.

In the meantime I could not find Tim Tom, who never left the camp except to follow me on walks. When he did not come to the mess tent for dinner, I knew something had happened. Tim Tom, as soon as he saw the staff putting on their kanzus, would rush to stand by my chair, so that he could be fed his favourite hot buttered toast, stamping his tiny feet impatiently if he thought there was unnecessary delay.

Stan kept trying to calm me down by saying he had probably found himself a mate. He had decided not to tell me until next morning that a leopard had taken Tim Tom and he was in a tree near the tent. I was in such despair when I heard the news that Stan insisted on taking me away from the camp for a few days. We went up to stay at Nanyuki, at the lovely Mount Kenya Safari Lodge.

CHAPTER

5

Kenya now had its independence and my friend Jomo Kenyatta was the new president. I met him through a friend of his, Major Erskine. Margaret Kenyatta was already one of my friends and at least in Kenya there were no race barriers. One had as many African friends as one did Indians and European friends. It was something one never thought about. In fact, I was offered a job by the new parliament, but my lifestyle did not suit being tied down, so I declined that commitment.

Up until now Ol Orion had been very isolated, and Tana was free to wander about the bush without any fear of predators. But now a dairy farmer had moved into the area and he threatened to shoot Tana the next time she came through his farm, as he said the male lions were causing all his cattle to abort. I was in such a panic; I could not lock my beloved Tana up nor could I tell her where to go and where not go, so I employed a Masai warrior to accompany her. She was so famous by this time that two countries offered to take her, but this would have meant a zoo situation and I would never have let her live in a zoo.

I decided that just as Joy and George Adamson had managed to establish their lioness, Elsa, in the wild, as Joy wrote in her famous book *Born Free*, so I would do the same with Tana. The problems were numerous, but finally Ted Goss, a very famous game warden, came to my rescue and agreed to take her. Ted had taken over the first African District Council Game Reserve in the Meru district. It was on the foothills of Mount Kenya and stretched all the way to the Somaliland border.

I then asked Carr Hartley, who was famous in Kenya for his capturing of wild animals for various zoos around the world, to give me a pride of lions to take down with Tana as she would not be able to survive on her own. Carr was wonderfully generous, refusing to let me buy the lions from him. His sister Diana, a great friend of mine, had been killed by a lion, and the least he could do, he said, was to help establish a wild pride in her memory.

The terrible day came when I had to take Tana up to Carr's farm and leave her there, so that she could be gradually introduced to her new pride. It was the first time we had ever been separated and I was so anxious.

On the morning of the release, we left early. I had on a jersey, and was sitting in the back of my safari car with my arms around my angel lioness, tears pouring down my cheeks and wetting her fur. When we arrived at the river and I had to leave her, I felt as if my life were coming to an end. Tana, feeling my despair, had taken my jersey in her teeth and was trying to prevent me from leaving; I had to pull her mouth open to get her to release me. The other lions were in their containers on the back of one of Stan's lorries. Ted Goss had organised a kill for them to be left with.

In a flood of tears I drove back to Ted's camp, where I had my own tent. Tana and I had stayed here together for a few days while we had looked for the ideal place to release her and her new pride. That night I was lying alone in my bed, in total despair at not having my adored Tana beside me, when I heard the grunts of a hunting lion. It reminded me so much of my beloved that I was sobbing away, when the flaps of the tent opened and Tana threw herself on top of me. In her excitement and ecstasy at finding her mother, the whole tent collapsed. Tana had deserted the pride that I had gone to so much trouble to find for her, because she preferred to be with me.

So I decided to move to Meru and live there with her. Ted Goss said I could come back and 'stop bothering him on the radio telephone' if I would build a lodge there. My mother was in India with Rory at the time, so my great friend Solange de la Bruyere, now Solange Batsell Herter, who was staying with me, lent me the money so that it could all be arranged as soon as possible. The result was that I built a lodge on the banks of the Rojewero River, in the Tana Basin. Ted gave me 40 prisoners, and together we learned through trial and error how to build a lodge using the natural products of the area. It was an unforgettable experience.

I had chosen to build on the banks of the Rojewero River because it was so picturesque with the semi-desert in front and the magnificent snow-capped Mount Kenya in the distance and then behind us were some densely wooded forests and valleys. It was truly beautiful and I loved the isolation. I was in my early thirties and I was the only white woman in the entire area and 35 miles away from Ted Goss's camp. I lived on a compass point, with a radio telephone that worked for one hour a day and was my only access to the outside world. Stan was mostly on safari with clients, but gave me the use of some of his safari lorries as there were no roads, only elephant tracks, so provisions and building materials had to be brought in once a week.

In between safaris, Stan came and saw to the technical side of things, like sanitation, pumps and electricity which I had to run off a generator. I built the lodge out of bamboo, with fan-like makuti palm leaf thatching for the roof. Inside, there was a large sitting room and a dining room. Outside was a large terrace where we enjoyed many evenings soaking in the evening sunlight and enjoying the solitude. Stan built a swimming pool nearby as the river was teeming with crocodiles. Sleeping quarters were individual bungalows, with four-poster beds also made out of bamboo. All the bamboo walls and beds were varnished and I used the local beautifully patterned cottons for all the curtains. Every time I went to Meru, a six-hour drive away, I would collect the lovely local tapestry work, with which I decorated the walls.

My brother Caryll, not surprisingly, made me build an airstrip on the flat piece of ground on the other side of the river. I was very proud of myself as I built a causeway across the river to get to the airstrip, which all my beloved elephants then used, much to my delight.

I was further delighted when David Hicks, who was at the time I would say England's most famous interior decorator, came down on a visit with my mother and Rory. I had known him and his lovely wife Pamela, the Earl of Mountbatten's daughter, since the days of the South of France, where he was a frequent visitor. David took photographs of my lodge, which I had named Kenmare after my mother, and he then wrote an article about it, which appeared in the *Tatler* magazine.

Kenmare soon appeared on the map of Kenya and that area, which stretched all the way to the Somaliland border, was subsequently named Kenmare, after my mother. Tana and I used to walk East Africa together. Because we were so well known, the tribesmen gave me the name of Toto ya Simba, child of the lion.

Before going to Meru I had taken a course in first aid and learnt about all the basic medicines and their usage. Thanks goodness I did this, as it was of great benefit. The distance between the lodge and the nearest habitation was such that in an emergency I would need to be able to handle most situations until I could get help. After the first aid course I bullied my doctor, William Boyle, into teaching me as much home-doctoring as possible. When I left Nairobi I took drugs, pills, potions and copious notes, with a veritable arsenal of medical supplies. I found studying medicine fascinating and as I progressed I was able to handle most of the simple illnesses, wounds and minor complaints. I was the local doctor, and also the most favoured witch doctor, as Tana and I spent our time undoing all the curses put on the tribesmen by the witchdoctors. They would walk for miles to see us – my life was simply magical!

Each day I used to wake up with Tana beside me in my tent, never knowing what the day would bring or what adventure we would be embarking on that day. My adored lioness, who had adopted my way of life and later taught me hers, even to this day I still feel she is beside me looking after me. She was so wonderfully loving and protective of me, lying with her great head on the pillow beside me at night with one of her heavy paws across my chest. Tana could pick up my every emotion, as I could pick up hers.

Sometimes she used to disappear for a few days at a time. I and my wonderful Somali tracker Mahomet would always find her and check that she was all right. She had made her own choice of mates and found herself a yellow-maned frontier lion, rather ugly in comparison to my handsome black-maned choice, I thought, but I had to respect her decision! It was so marvellous; the day she produced her cubs, she tried to carry them back to me but I would not let her. I drove her and the first of the two little cubs back to her new pride and told her sternly that she had to stay away. She looked at me with those pathetic large golden eyes, as if to say, 'What have I done wrong this time?' I explained that this was her new life and she must stay put, but that I would be with her every day.

Every morning Mahomet would walk out into the bush and locate her, then he and I would go in my International safari car and give them large hunks of meat – this was strictly forbidden by Ted Goss, so obviously we kept quiet about it. As soon as she heard the safari car arriving she would appear and jump into the front seat with me. There would then be lots of hugging and kissing, while Mahomet forked out the meat. Then I would take her huge paw, kiss it all over, which was my message that I was saying goodbye for the day.

Whenever this happened, Tana would jump out and go back to her pride. I wept every night as I was always so worried that something might happen to her. She had spent so many years of her life lying beside me, that I would keep reaching out for her, to find the bed bare. Stan on the other hand was delighted and when he visited he used to say, 'Thank God that bloody lioness has finally left. At last I can share a bed with you and I don't have to worry about landing on top of a lion when I am making love to you!'

* * *

In 1963, a couple of years after I arrived in Meru, the Shifta war broke out. The Shifta, so named by the Kenyan government after the Somali word for bandit, were attempting to create a greater Somalia. They objected to being ruled by what they considered an inferior tribe, the Kikuyu. The war was particularly brutal and very quickly the Shifta began killing all foreign tribesmen.

I was one of the first people to know that war had broken out, as the survivors had come to me for treatment. The area became very dangerous; the Shifta were inclined to bury people alive, head first with their legs sticking out. Sometimes, if we were lucky, we would get there in time to dig them out alive. Amongst the famous people that were killed was the wonderful George Adamson. I realised that most of my beloved staff were now at serious risk. I begged them to leave me, but none of them would, they were so intensely loyal. They would have given their lives for me.

I did not feel I was in any danger, but there were other forces working to tear me away from Meru. Beryl Markham, who by this point had become a fixed feature in our lives, was Kenya's top race-horse trainer at the time, and was training Mummy's racehorses. She, Charles Norman and Jan Thane had hatched a plan to buy a farm in South Africa where Beryl would train racehorses while Jan started a dairy farm. Beryl had been working on my mother to join them, telling her about the dangerous lifestyle of her beloved daughter. Finally she managed to persuade my doctor to speak to my mother on her next visit.

William Boyle was a brilliant doctor and a most remarkable man. He used to spend his time stitching me up as I was always rescuing animals and being scratched or bitten by them. He was forever lecturing me on my dangerous lifestyle. He had over the years taken care of Joseph as well as Tana or whatever animal needed medical treatment at the time. Tana would always accompany me, as did

Joseph, when I needed to see Dr Boyle. Both of them adored him. I think perhaps it was because he always kept sweets for Joseph and some meaty chicken bones for Tana. The faces of his clients in the waiting room as I entered with a huge lioness and a chimp were always priceless, though no one ever objected. But as I have said before, all things were possible in Kenya in those days. Nowadays, in South Africa, if I take my chimp or baboons to my beloved Dr Anderson I am rushed into a private room so as not to upset his clients any more than they are already at the sight of this crazy woman and her animals.

I had been resisting all efforts on Beryl's part to get Mummy to look at the farm in South Africa; she had in fact been trying to talk my mother into it for a couple of years. My mother was visiting from France and this time William called me into his office and said, 'Pat, I have to speak to you about your mother. I do not think you realise that Enid has a bad heart and the altitude of Kenya is very bad for her. As long as you remain in Kenya, your mother will always visit and you are quite simply putting her life at risk by staying here.'

He did not stop there. 'I believe Beryl has found a beautiful farm in South Africa at sea level. I know how much you love your mother; this means that you will have to choose between her health and your love of Kenya and your crazy animals. It will also save me having to write out your death certificate, as your totally lunatic lifestyle cannot continue much longer. If the Shifta don't kill you, one of those wild animals that you insist upon rescuing certainly will. I have had enough of sewing and patching you up.'

It was not until I got back to Ol Orion and had time to think over what William had told me that I realised the full implications. When faced with the fact that I might be instrumental in causing my mother's death, I had no option. The love I had for this beautiful fragile being mattered more than anything else in my life. She was all things to me, my child, my mother and my friend, and without her I felt my world would have ceased to exist.

I know William believed my mother had a serious heart problem and certainly she found breathing difficult when she was in Kenya. In fact, she did not have a bad heart; she was simply allergic to the medicine that the doctor in France had prescribed for her arthritis. We found this out later when living in South Africa where the brilliant Dr Teperson in Somerset West treated her – and so her life was saved. Maybe fate as well as Beryl had taken a hand.

I agreed to go with Mummy to look at the farm Beryl had found. She had painted a magnificent picture of the historic farmhouse with the Helderberg behind, overlooking Gordon's Bay, and the green paddocks in front filled with beautiful thoroughbreds. That night, when I got Mummy on her own, I squashed any ideas she might have had of purchasing yet another farm. 'Darling,' she said, 'you are such a little spoilsport. There is no harm in just having a look.'

South Africa was so sophisticated in comparison to Kenya, with wonderful tarmac roads everywhere. The farm was beautiful, but it was rather like being back at Cap Ferrat, overlooking the Mediterranean, where everything was rather treeless and tidy. The towns were proper towns, with no lovely African markets teeming and bustling with life. The villages were proper villages, with beautiful Cape Dutch and colonial houses, all beautifully painted. What I could not accept were the signs everywhere telling you where blacks were and were not allowed. This even included queues at post offices and banks and the like. I had never seen anything like it in my life and was horrified!

This country was not my beloved Africa, there was no wildlife on the sides of the road, no waiting for elephant to cross, no huge tropical forests, no exotic tribesmen with spears and paint. All the Africans wore shabby European clothing. Then there was another group of people referred to as the Cape Coloureds, they were also treated as Africans and were not allowed to consort with the whites. Except, I am sure, that a lot of the female staff, black or Coloured, made their way to the master's bedroom at night. The racial rules of separation were utterly ridiculous!

Nevertheless, Mummy bought Broadlands, the farm Beryl had found. By the time we returned to Kenya, she had signed an option and paid a deposit.

At first, I would come down from Kenya and spend the time with Mummy when she was at Broadlands. Two or three months was enough for me, and then I would rush back to be with Tana and Joseph, and that wonderful sense of freedom surrounded by magnificent country, tribes and wild animals. I also used to see Stan, who had changed his attitude about wild animals. I think getting to know Tana, Tim Tom and Joseph and seeing how wonderful and faithful they were and how Tana had saved my life, finally persuaded him to quit hunting and take out only photographic safaris. I refused to marry him; he had a son and a daughter he adored and I was not going to break up a family. Like all the local safari hunters, Stan was a notorious womaniser, so in having an affair with him I was not doing anything different from the affairs he was having with his lady clients on safari – the facts of which he was never shy to share with me in detail.

In 1968, my mother finally decided to move to South Africa permanently, so I had to leave everything I loved. The day before I left for good, I went to say goodbye and was crying so hard that I could hardly see where I was going. Instead of first jumping on the bonnet, Tana leaped into the car beside me. She could feel my despair and had come to comfort me. She had always been part of me, part of my life, part of my Africa. Through her love and guidance I had learned to live with nature, to become part of this lovely country and its wonderful people. She had taught me her life, and I had taught her mine – saying goodbye was truly heartbreaking.

My years with both Tana and Stan were the most wonderful years of my life. Tana shared my bed at night as well as my thoughts and my dreams. We did not have to be in the same room to pick up each other's emotions. Now I had come to say goodbye, I threw my arms around her neck, the tears pouring down my cheeks into the soft fur of my beloved lioness. She put her huge paw over me; she knew my feelings of misery. This was to be the last time we would be together and it was unbearable. I knew I had to leave, I could not keep her from her cubs any longer and I had to get back to Nairobi, as I was leaving the next day. Giving her one last hug and covering her magnificent face with kisses, I told her to leave. She jumped down, looking back at me once as she returned to her cubs; her beautiful eyes, so sad, were reaching out to me, bidding me farewell, she knew. I drove away in utter despair; it was the worst moment of my life.

I arranged to meet Stan at Mombasa with my car and dogs, ready to board a ship for Durban. It was to be my last trip with the man I loved. My life of glamour, romance and passion was coming to an end.

My mother kept my farm at Karen for four years, with Mutete who had been my cook in charge of the staff. Lane had now become the Broadlands kennel maid and had already left Kenya with Mummy's 10 dogs. My adored chimpanzee Joseph had been given to a friend of Stan's who had a large farm at Kilimanjaro. A few years after Tanganyika got its independence a lot of farms were taken over and while I tried to find out what had happened to Joseph, I never did. To this day, the memory of Joseph and what could have been his fate still haunts me. That is why, this time, I am making sure that the future of Kalu, my chimpanzee in South Africa, along with all my baboons and monkeys, is assured – well after my death.

BROADLANDS

CHAPTER

1

When I first laid eyes on the famous Broadlands Stud Farm I had to admit that it was incredibly beautiful, despite my reservations about leaving Kenya. Lying on the slopes of the valley was the loveliest eighteenth-century farmhouse imaginable. The driveway led you past low whitewashed walls with purple agapanthus and their display of welcoming colour. Expansive green paddocks stretched beyond the driveway and grazing horses added to the picture-perfect scene. The stable yard was enormous and various cottages, barns and silos filled the estate. Looking down over the azure waters of False Bay, one's view of blue vistas was interrupted only by the green bank of established vineyards that bordered the lower part of the farm.

False Bay is well known for the 'south-easter' or 'Cape Doctor' – a brisk to gale-force breeze which is believed to blow all lingering germs away. The name of the bay arose from the number of clipper ships that once steered off course believing they were headed for Cape Town's harbour, only to be thrust into the bay by fierce winds and often ending fatefully on rocky ground. Broadlands was truly beautiful, almost too picture perfect – after so many happy years in the Kenyan bush it reminded me of the South of France.

At the top of the farm were the horses, living on an already well-established stud farm with sweeping views down to the beach, where they would head each day for their early-morning gallop. To get there we had to cross what is now the N2 – a national freeway that is today choked with daily traffic. Later we built an additional stable yard which stood at the foothills of the mountains, close to the sea.

Before it got its present name, Broadlands was called De Fortuin or Fortuinje and was the last outpost on the wagon road before the treacherous track called the Hottentots-Holland Kloof Pass that led one over the mountains. Records say that the first crossing was in 1664; by 1821 during the 'Great Trek' of Afrikaner farmers to the interior there were as many as 4 500 ox-wagons attempting the crossing each year. The route was so treacherous that apparently only one in five of the wagons made it through without damage, with many plunging fatefully back down the mountain.

When Mummy and I first lived at Broadlands, one could still see the spot where they used to winch the ox-wagons over the pass. Today's traffic on the four-lane N2 zig-zags its way up Sir Lowry's Pass at tremendous speeds, oblivious to the struggles of past generations to reach the other side.

At sunset, this mountainous pass would turn bright pink and the beautiful bay and beaches would take on a fiery glow. Gradually, as the moon came up, the reflection in the usually calm waters of the bay would turn the sea to silver, with the dark outlines of Table Mountain and Cape Point in the background framing this incredible picture of scenic beauty.

Mummy was utterly thrilled with the beauty, so despite my reservations about leaving my beloved Kenya, I did what I had to do and joined her there – although it did take me two years. As a compromise I used to accompany her to Broadlands on her three-month yearly visits from the South of France.

The acquisition of Broadlands was initially through Beryl Markham's machinations and was intended to be in partnership with her present and past lovers, Jan Thane and Charles Norman. Back in Kenya, Beryl had been living on Charles's farm and training and riding his horses. Her affections were quickly transferred when Jan, who was quite a bit younger, came from Denmark to work as farm manager. But when Jan met another woman and Beryl found this out she confronted him in the Muthaiga Club in Nairobi with a horse whip, chasing him from his gin and tonic into the car park where she whipped him black and blue while demanding he end his liaison. From here a complex web of action began – Beryl wanted Jan as far from his new lady friend as possible, Jan wanted Beryl and her horse whip as far from Kenya as possible and so the farce of leaving Kenya began. And one in which Mummy and I were to play a central role.

As time passed it became evident that the male contingent in the Beryl trio never had any intention of staying in South Africa and had in fact used the whole thing as a ploy to get the feisty Beryl as far from Kenya as they could. Charles was supposed to have paid half but at the time, and after all the promises, he had some reason as to why he was not able to do so. Needless to say, none of the partnerships were ever realised. Mummy was left buying Broadlands and financing the entire removal of Beryl and her racing establishment. To top it all, as soon as Beryl was truly settled at Broadlands and Mummy and I were there, Jan beetled back off to Kenya and married his new girlfriend, leaving us an enraged Beryl to deal with.

Life from this point on was certainly never dull at Broadlands; we grew the farm into a world-famous stud and along with this came a colourful history to look back on. Sadly, things at Broadlands are very different today – largely due to my own rather naive trusting nature, or what I often refer to as my stupidity. But back then when the French champagne still flowed and caviar was the order of the day, we went from glory to glory in the racing world and what a wonderful life it was!

* * *

The farm was certainly full: Buster Parnell, the champion jockey in Kenya, had come over and was established in one of the other houses with his family. The Kramers, from whom Mummy had bought Broadlands, were still living in the main house, and John their son managed the vineyards at the bottom of the farm as well as their horses in the stud section.

Mummy, who had ridden and been with horses and racehorses all her life, found Broadlands had become her ideal home rather than La Fiorentina. I think something else that really sold the property to her was a large, perfectly flat area of grass to the side that would need no alteration to make a croquet lawn. When she was told that there was a thriving croquet club in the area, I knew that did it.

Mummy was a brilliant player and although there was a croquet lawn at Fiorentina nobody had ever played with any enthusiasm. It wasn't one of the games of the Côte d'Azur. It was a hangover from her Australian upbringing. All the Lindemans played croquet and although Mummy had tried to instil in us a love of the game, only Caryll was a willing participant.

Despite having settled in at Broadlands, I missed Kenya dreadfully. After four years of living in South Africa, Mummy sold Ol Orion, my beautiful house at Karen, so I transferred my yearly visit to my wonderful friends the Blocks, who owned Tree Tops and most of the other better-known safari lodges. Tubby's father had arrived in Kenya many years before with not much more than a wheelbarrow of goods to sell – so by all accounts, the Block family did very well for themselves in Kenya. My South African friends and I often used to descend upon Tubby and his wife Aino and we always had the most marvellous time. They had a lovely big house in Muthaiga – a very smart area just a couple of miles north of Nairobi's city centre. The area had beautiful shady streets and was thick with trees and birdlife. The house had magnificent views of the descending valley and distant mountains. We would usually stay here for three or four days before heading out to their magnificent farm at Naivasha in the Rift Valley. From here we would fly to different safari camps where we would then spend up to a month in utter bliss in bush teeming with wildlife and well away from the worries of the world.

Tubby Block has now sadly passed away, and Aino lives in London – a far cry from the freedom of the Kenyan bush she felt was home. We are cheered, however, by her many visits to Broadlands and she remains a deeply treasured friend of mine.

* * *

After Jan's desertion, Beryl lost all interest in Broadlands. The last thing in the world she wanted was to end up on a fairly isolated farm with three other women – that is, myself, Mummy and her secretary, Julia – for company and not a man in sight. The horses she brought from Kenya did reasonably well: Mountie, Lone Eagle and Fair Realm all won a number of races. But she spent her time cooking the books – one of her many unfortunate habits – as well as being rude to Mummy. In Kenya, she once stole all my staff wages that I had just been to the bank to collect and then another time she stole my new camera. But Beryl was Beryl and a law unto herself: we largely learnt to live with this.

Finally, Beryl took her own horses and left Broadlands to set up a training establishment at Eerste River, an area not far from Broadlands, but still a fair distance from Cape Town. After two years, she gave up and took herself and her horses to Rhodesia, as Zimbabwe was then called. She was gradually working her way back to Kenya, where she passed away in Nairobi in 1986 at the age of 83. Her later years were lived largely in poverty, with assistance given to her by friends for whom she had trained.

Life was certainly a little calmer with Beryl no longer at Broadlands. I adored Buster Parnell; it was lovely having him and his wife and two children on the farm, but unfortunately there was not enough opportunity for a great jockey like him on Broadlands at the time. I had not started training as yet and there were only a few racehorses. Buster finally returned to his native Ireland, where he became champion jockey

Jimmy McKeon, a young Englishman, then became our jockey. At this stage we had about 20 horses and a work rider was also needed. Luckily the stipendiary steward at Kenilworth came to the rescue and recommended Shelagh McCutcheon, who had been riding work for Beryl. Shelagh would come from Cape Town every morning and ride work for us. She was a very tall, slim, good-looking blonde and a wonderful horsewoman. She turned out to be an absolute treasure and has been living with us at Broadlands ever since.

We needed a trainer and Mummy knew someone who had been working for the Delamere family – the family that had been so prominent in the founding of colonial Kenya. Ray Groombridge settled in with his family, but after a few months of his training methods, I was in despair. He himself was a nice man and might have been with horses all his life, but he was not a horseman; his feeding programme was dreadful and he did not have the necessary respect for his horses. South Africa had some top-class trainers and he was just not in their league. Mummy and I had gone to the sales each year and had bought a number of very promising yearlings, but despite this, I could see we would not get anywhere with him in control.

It was around this time that Frank, my first husband, read about me in one of the Sydney papers and got in touch with me. This turn of events proved to be most favourable for the Broadlands Stud and for myself, and I like to think for Frank too.

What was amazing is that just prior to this I had been very worried about my mother's health, and a chemist friend of ours, Moishe Rome, had suggested that I take her to a famous faith healer, a Mrs van der Wat. I waited in the car while Mummy went to see her. Mrs Van, as it turned out, was a medium as well as a faith healer and she started telling Mummy about me. She said, 'You have a daughter and white light shines between the two of you. She has a yellow dog with yellow eyes (this was Rogue, one of my rescued Bahamians) and I see a man coming towards her from a faraway country beginning with "A", I think it is Australia, and they are explaining to me: it is like an old coat that becomes new.' About six months later, Frank arrived from Australia at my invitation and Rory greeted him at the airport with, 'Hello, old coat!'

TOP LEFT: My father, General
Frederick 'Caviar' Cavendish,
was Commanding General
at Aldershot at the time of
my birth. A highly decorated
cavalry officer, he was also a
10-goal polo player and he
lived his life upon a horse.

TOP RIGHT: My mother,
born Enid Lindeman of the
Australian wine family, quite
simply the most incredible
and loving mother one could
wish for!

LEFT: Engaged in the Bahamas.
From left: My fiancé Richard
Murphy holding one of my
rescued poodles, me, Richard's
father, who was Governor
of the Bahamas, and Lady
Murphy.

ABOVE: The St Hospice point of St Jean Cap Ferrat peninsula curves to face the mainland over the Bay of Beaulieu. Not content with just La Fiorentina, a huge Florentine-style mansion, the jealous Lord Furness had bought all the neighbouring houses as well to keep would-be lovers away from his beautiful wife.

LEFT: Scene of many lunch parties at one of Furness's houses on Cap St Hospice.

OPPOSITE PAGE:

TOP LEFT: Though a fashion icon of her times, Enid was completely lacking in vanity.

TOP RIGHT: Enid by the popular Surrealist painter Leonor Fini, who began painting portraits in Monte Carlo in 1940. We saw a lot of her at La Fiorentina – she was very glamorous and always arrived accompanied by two boyfriends, one fair and one dark.

BOTTOM LEFT: Pat at the age of 20, by Anthony Armstrong-Jones. The precious photograph is much the worse for an encounter with one of my baboons!

BOTTOM RIGHT: Enid in one of the innumerable gardens at Burrough Court, Lord Furness's Victorian mansion.

TOP: Part of the entrance hall at La Fiorentina, with glimpses of connecting rooms.

BOTTOM: My wonderful brother Rory, who lived for beautiful things.

TOP: White cats in bowl: I hope Rory would have approved such a juxtaposition of art and life, though my rescued animals seldom show much respect for the rare china on display at Broadlands.

BOTTOM: Tim Tom, my rescued Thomson's gazelle, accompanied me everywhere – even on safari.

TOP LEFT: My beloved lion Tana, always part of my life, part of my Africa.

TOP RIGHT: Tana liked to lie on the roof at Ol Orion, and when she was not asleep in the shade she kept an eye on what was going on down below.

LEFT: When I had to leave her, I felt as if my life were coming to an end. Tana, feeling my despair, took my jersey in her teeth and tried to prevent me from leaving.

CHAPTER

2

I was in my early twenties when I first married Frank O'Neill and he was a year younger. We had met on the *Orcades*, a ship going out to Australia. It was 1949 and I was accompanying Mummy on yet another Australian voyage. My younger brother Caryll was also with us, but he was disembarking at Port Said in order to return to his farming ventures in Kenya. After an eternity of seasickness, Mummy and I were finally well enough to dress for dinner and as we descended the very grand staircase that led into the dining room, Frank saw us and could not look away. In those days when travelling on a liner one had to wear full evening dress, and if

Frank's memory is correct I wore a white evening dress that night, while Mummy wore her glittering diamonds.

Frank was on his way home from time spent swimming in both England and Europe and was sitting at a table with his 'mates'. As he told me later, he had a bet with them that 'he would have that beautiful girl in bed before the end of the voyage'. He did, and then the following year we announced our engagement. This caused a huge thing in the Australian press. 'Swimmer to marry English heiress,' blazed the headlines.

Frank was a penniless young man; his father was the keeper of the Manly Baths, so it was no surprise that he was brought up in the water and became an Australian Olympic swimming champion. The family home was a flat over the Manly Baths and it was here that Frank's training was supervised by his father. He would swim five miles a day and then move on to an hour of water polo, massage and water ballet. He was also a keen surfer, although his father discouraged this as it built the wrong type of muscles for swimming. He became the first man in the world to break a minute and he captained the Australian Olympic team at Helsinki in 1952, competing in the 100 metres freestyle, 100 metres backstroke and the 200 metres freestyle relay.

Once we had announced the engagement we all headed back to France, stopping along the way to visit Caryll in Kenya and then on to see friends in England, before finally arriving home at Cap Ferrat in the South of France.

We got married at the British Consulate in Nice on 30 September 1950. I did not want a church wedding. I had never really wanted to get married, I never wanted to leave my mother and my family and I did not like the feeling of being trapped, which a church wedding would have given me. I had been engaged several times before, but had always broken it off before the wedding day got too close.

I enjoyed my marriage to Frank immensely; he taught me to swim properly, so that I could accompany him on his long training sessions. I would wear flippers, which helped me keep up, so every day we would swim across the Bay of Beaulieu, as La Fiorentina's harbour was on the bay. Once through my goggles I thought I saw a submarine but it turned out to be a huge whale I was almost swimming beside. It was very deep and cold in the middle of the bay and on several occasions there were naval ships anchored out there. Nearer to land, it was quite beautiful. One would swim over and look down on the shelving valleys of the underwater land mass. It was rather like the Barrier Reef, with exotic fish, mountains and valleys formed by the rock formations and all types of underwater ferns and plants waving in the slight movement of the Mediterranean.

It was during these swims that I learned to love lobsters; until then they had been my favourite food. They lived in caves in the rocks and used to decorate their little homes with coloured glass and things they picked off the sea bed; they would even have mating dances and hold claws. From then on I could never eat lobsters again.

Frank was good looking and had immense charm and when he was out of the water he turned his attention to the ladies. He adored the ladies and of course they adored him. We had the funniest marriage as all my friends fell for him. As being faithful was not on his agenda, most weekends he would spend with one of them. In fact, sex was what had won Frank his first world swimming record. He fell in love with one of the ladies competing in another event and she said she would only go to bed with him if he broke the record. So he did, and they did! He said to me that the effort nearly killed him, but all he could think about was the reward!

I had been raised on my mother's precepts – 'Never be afraid, never be ill and if you are don't talk about it and above all never be jealous' – and as I was not jealous, Frank had no need to hide his numerous peccadilloes. In the end, after about four years, we only got divorced because I had fallen for another man. Frank wasn't at all keen on getting divorced; the marriage offered him some measure of protection from numerous adoring women all wanting to wed him. One of them was a Mrs Mann who was living in the South of France. She even went as far as to ask me to divorce Frank so that she could marry him. Frank however wasn't the least bit interested in either a new wife or a divorce.

When we were first married, Frank used to go back to Australia every year for the swimming carnivals, while I would go with my mother to her house in Nassau. The house was on the edge of the beach and I would spend my time swimming and water-skiing – other than riding and driving, these were two of my most pleasurable pursuits.

Dancing was another passion of mine, having loved ballet as a child and later Miss Varcarnis's ballroom dancing classes in London. Nassau with its lovely calypso music and great nightclubs was where I would spend my nights. I became their champion limbo dancer and I found out later that the habitués would have bets on me – as I was thin and very athletic, I was able to keep dancing and get under the bar only a few inches from the ground.

* * *

It was on one of these nights that I first saw Aymon. Clarissa Chaplain, a long-time friend of mine, was staying with us in Nassau at the time. We were both in the nightclub with friends when we saw a gorgeous young man come onto the dance floor. Not only was he tall and good-looking, but he had a dachshund draped over one shoulder.

Clarissa and I, almost with one breath, said, 'Why don't we ever meet anyone that looks like that and loves dogs?'

The following night Clarissa was going to a cocktail party and I really did not want to go with her. I hated the compulsory small-talk, and like my mother I had a strong distaste for alcohol. A glass or two of champagne was the utmost I could manage. Smoking of course was a different matter; I was already a chain smoker and looking back, this may have been one of the reasons why I was so hyperactive.

Anyhow, Clarissa finally persuaded me to join her. It was at a house further down Cable Beach and as we walked into the sitting room the first person we saw, standing by the mantelpiece, was the beautiful young man from the night before.

I think, as with my previous loves, it was love at first sight. He came straight over to me and said, 'I saw you at the nightclub last night. You were so beautiful I could not stop thinking about you – and here you are tonight; my dream comes true.'

From then on we were inseparable. I could never have a sexual relationship with anyone unless I was in love. I had lots of male friends and dancing partners but these relationships never went further.

This was the first man I had fallen in love with since Frank. Only a few weeks went by before he was begging me to marry him. Mummy, meanwhile, had hired a detective to get evidence of Frank's infidelities. The funny side of this story was that the lawyers had hired a female detective and the upshot was that she fell for Frank and started an affair with him herself. She was therefore not prepared to provide the evidence needed.

Yet despite this, Frank was still not keen on a divorce and so Mummy bought me a house in Florida where she, Aymon and I went to live for three months. At the end of this time we were deemed to be 'residents' and could apply for my much-needed divorce.

Aymon, who was half-American and half-French, was known as Count Aymon de Roussy de Sales. We got married in a registry office in New York. Once again I did not want a church wedding, but this time I did not make a run for it! Aymon was seven years younger than me, he was 21 and I was 28 at the time we were married. I never really noticed the difference in age; he was a very worldly young man and also a great lover of women. One of his ex-girlfriends had already written a book about him called *Chocolates for Breakfast*. So you can well imagine what a treat I was in for!

Mummy bought me a flat in New York, where Aymon and I stayed for a while. I had my three rescue dogs from the Bahamas with me – Rogue, Smokey and Bandit. They eventually travelled all over the world with me and ended up in their old age in South Africa. I soon decided that I could not live in New York, as I was too far away from my beloved mother and Rory, so I took Aymon back to the South of France. He loved it there and we would then go back to New York and Nassau every year. We also, along with my mother, went to visit my younger brother Caryll on his farm in Kenya, where my mother had built a house for us both. Life was nothing short of blissful during these days of travel and love.

Not long after we were married, Aymon and I were spending a weekend in London with a friend of mine. We were playing bridge when I felt a terrible searing pain in my abdomen. I made an excuse and quietly went to bed, all the while remembering my mother's edict, '… never be jealous, never be afraid and never be ill, and if you are don't complain'. By morning, however, I was in such enormous agony that I asked the hostess to call my mother.

My mother called her doctor in London, Dr Goldman. I had an ectopic pregnancy, but had left it so long that by the time they got me to hospital, my lungs had collapsed and I had practically bled to death and was unconscious. After this I was never able to have children, but it was all meant to be, as if I had been a mother I could never have led the magical life that I did with my lioness in Kenya, and this is a life I would not have traded for the world.

We returned to the South of France, but I was not feeling well enough to go home with Aymon to New York so he returned home alone. He had been gone several months when I received a letter from him, saying that he had found someone else and would like a divorce. I readily agreed to this and a few months later, I stopped in New York on my way to Nassau to arrange for the sale of the apartment.

On the night before I was due to leave for Nassau to meet my mother, Aymon heard I was in New York, and called me up and said he wanted to see me. We went out to dinner and then ended up spending the night together. He was still asleep as I got dressed in the morning. I had to leave early for the airport and he awoke as I was about to leave. Just as I opened the door, a naked Aymon leaped out of bed and begged me not to go, saying the divorce was all a terrible mistake and he still loved me. I had to catch my plane, so I left Aymon lying on the floor trying to cling to my departing ankle as he begged me not to leave him. That was the last time I saw my beautiful Aymon, who later developed his artistic talent and became a well-known artist. Years later, once I was living in South Africa, he sent me two of his paintings and once again begged me to remarry him.

* * *

Strangely enough, Aymon and Frank crossed paths with one another once again on their return into my life many years later –
during that time Frank reignited our relationship and asked me to
remarry him; so too did Aymon, but by then Frank had hot-footed
his way over to South Africa from Australia – so on 17 November
1970 we were re-married, this time in Kenya in a Registry Office.
It was not however without cold feet on my part and Mummy and
Rory spent a good deal of time at Lake Naivasha talking me into it.
Just prior to the event, Caryll, whom Mummy had flown over from
England for the event, rowed me out into the lake and spent about
three hours paddling amongst the hippos while persuading me not
to call the wedding off. His reassurances paid off and I married
Frank once again.

CHAPTER

3

Following the wedding, Frank and I spent three months in Australia. Mummy came too but rented a house with her staff while I stayed in Frank's lovely house at Manly, right on the beach, with a magnificent swimming pool. Being in Australia gave Mummy and me a perfect excuse to attend the Easter Sales in Sydney. It was here that I persuaded Mummy and Frank to buy a few yearlings. Among them was a filly that I named My Lovely, who later became the Cape's champion two-year-old. It was from this point that Australian stock began to play a significant role in the success of Broadlands.

These Australian imports soon began to cause much consternation in South Africa. The Jockey Club approached my mother and asked her not to import any more Australian yearlings, claiming that they would only lower the South African thoroughbred standard. Mummy of course paid no attention and year after year from these supposedly inferior imports I managed to train South African champion race fillies. Later, the progeny of these imported brood mares won every major black type race in the country. Thanks too to the fact that I had acquired some champion sires, namely Royal Prerogative, Averof and Marazion. Black type, by the way, refers to the bold type used in sales catalogues to indicate a horse that has won or placed in stakes races.

Back at Broadlands, Ray Groombridge had thankfully left and Adrian Coetzee, with his lovely wife and child, had moved into residence. Adrian had once been a jockey and had now moved into training. Arriving back from Australia with our new yearlings, Adrian immediately took on the training of My Lovely – but no man, particularly in South Africa, wants to have a woman breathing down his neck and I could not keep away from the stables. Shortly after this Adrian decided to leave – although today, Shelagh assures me he was going to leave despite me.

The morning after he had handed his notice in to Mummy I went into her bedroom. She sat up in bed and said to me, 'Pat, you either keep away from the stables, which I know is asking the impossible, or you train for me yourself.'

This idea of my mother's that her daughter would take over the training was met with utter horror at the Jockey Club of South Africa. A delegation of stewards led by her great friend Ivan Karie came to try and talk her out of it, saying they would give her a list of trainers who could train for her on the farm. As I said to Mummy, 'Terrance Millard, Syd Laird, or Theo de Klerk' (these being the top three trainers in South Africa at the time) 'are hardly likely to be on that list and I can almost guarantee you who will be on the list of no hopers they are going to present to you.' And with that I took the plunge and told her that I would take over the training of the horses and go to Australia and buy lovely yearling fillies that would go to stud later.

The Jockey Club could hardly refuse to accept me, but because I had a title and was the daughter of a millionaire, at the back of their minds I was just a society drone with communist leanings and they set about finding a way to stop me. Before granting me a trainer's licence, they made a special test for me to pass. It was six foolscap pages of questions plus the book of rules of the Jockey Club, which I needed to know off pat. I was told there would be a written test plus questions on the book of rules. I did not know what the written test would be about, but having had a cavalry general for a father who taught me to ride before I could walk, and along with my strict upbringing and contact with so many horses, from steeplechasers and hunters to polo ponies and Percherons as well some of the greatest race horses in the world, horses were what I knew best. Horses and animals had indeed been my life and for these reasons, the Jockey Club test was for me a mere formality.

On the day of my test, I arrived at the Jockey Club to be met by the head stipendiary steward, Mr Diamond. He was a tall man with a mop of silver hair and he ushered me into an empty room with a desk and told me I had three hours to complete the test. The pages included everything imaginable – a great deal of veterinary questions as well as questions on teeth, the names of the bones and the like. I was familiar with all the questions, having also spent my life with vets, farriers and people in this line of work. So far the test presented no difficulty. However one of the Jockey Club rules was written in such bad English it was hard to fathom the meaning. I therefore gave the written answer as it was in the book.

Within an hour and a half I was done and went into Mr Diamond's office. I will always remember his quizzical and somewhat amazed look, and how he said, 'You've got another hour and a half to finish the questions!'

I smiled and responded: 'Thank you very much, but I have finished. They were not difficult, but there is one question from the Jockey Club Book of Rules that does not make sense. Can you explain it to me? Just to be on the safe side I have given the correct answer as is written down.' Then when I pointed out the question, even he was puzzled about the way it was written. Later I heard from one of my friends that I got 99 per cent and that the stewards were laughing and all agreeing that I should have been given more farrier questions, but they conceded that even this would probably not have failed me. So, in the end, they had to give me my licence.

At that time in South Africa there were very few woman trainers in a very much male-dominated society. Jean Barnard was the talk of the country, and not only because it was rare to find a woman trainer, but also because she was eccentric and housed a lion in one of her stables. Tragically, Jean had a break-in at her home in Johannesburg and was shot four or five times – the injuries crippled her and today she lives in the United Kingdom.

When I first started training, a while before our yearly trips to Australia, I had gone with Mummy to the yearling sales in South Africa and bought colts and fillies. I had tried terribly hard to buy a colt called Harry Hotspur off one of the studs, having seen this outstanding colt in one of the paddocks. On being told roughly what his owner was hoping he would fetch I put in an offer, but the word that was returned to me was that the owner now doubted if she wanted to sell Harry Hotspur at all. My response then was to offer her whatever she wanted. Later I heard through the grapevine that she had said if the Countess (I was Countess de Roussy de Sales at the time, due to my marriage to Aymon) is so anxious to acquire him, he must have potential; I think therefore I will keep him and race him myself. Which she did, and he became a champion sprinter. I did not lose out entirely though and sent several of my mares to his sire, including Royal Affair – the product of which was Naughty Nymph, who was a great success.

*　*　*

With the new-found confidence I now had as an officially accepted and accredited trainer, I told Mummy that we were going to regularly buy yearling fillies in Sydney and that I would ask Tommy Smith, who to my mind is one of the greatest trainers in the world, to teach me his training methods. I also wanted to learn racing haematology from possibly the greatest equestrian vet in the world, Percy Sykes. He was one of the first veterinarians in the world to start conducting blood tests in order to measure a horse's response to training and he was in great demand. Percy did all of Tommy Smith's horses and he was a great friend of Frank's.

While we were in Sydney I would meet Tommy at the early-morning gallops. Gallops are common practice in racing the world over: before the heat of the day arrives and well before the horses need to eat, they are taken to the local racecourse to gallop and get accustomed to the grass track and the new surroundings. It's a magical part of the day, hearing the pounding of hooves and then seeing the horses emerge through the morning mist and come thundering past. Tommy was always marvellous to me and he and his lovely wife

Valerie became great friends – we would spend a lot of time together both at the races and in restaurants afterwards. Their daughter, the apple of their eyes – Gai Waterhouse, as she is now known – has since grown into a remarkable young woman and following in her father's footsteps is now one of Australia's top trainers,

Percy Sykes was also unbelievable with the sheer mountain of knowledge he was able to pass on to me. But perhaps there was a fair exchange going on, as my rally driving skills were put to good use travelling to the various stud farms around Sydney while Percy sat in the passenger seat with his nose buried in the piles of papers that accompanied him everywhere. This gave him more time to study his notes and gave me the opportunity to see some of the most wonderful Australian studs and their magnificent horses.

I arrived home more determined than ever to turn Broadlands into a world-class stud farm one day. The South African studs I had been to visit were all somewhat primitive in those days. Today, of course, things have changed dramatically, but back then I had been used to the magnificence of my stepfather's studs, Gilltown and Sandley, and then after seeing the lovely studs in Australia – well, South African studs had, in my mind, a long way to go.

To my horror, stallions in South Africa at this time were treated like wild beasts and kept locked in their stables all day; they only ever seemed to emerge from these dark walls for covering – this being the technical term used to describe a horse mating. By contrast, the mares and foals hardly ever saw a stable. They remained out in all weathers, with heavily matted tails and manes, and were never groomed. Indeed, these large fields of thoroughbreds looked more like something from the Wild West of North America than carefully bred horses. I was told at the time that the horses needed to be brought up 'tough' – this, people believed, had a strong correlation with the horse's speed.

Blood testing was a novelty in this country at the time, and to my vast surprise in England too. While visiting some famous English trainers there, I spoke at length about racing haematology and what a difference it was making to my training methods. None of them had ever heard about it and they were not the slightest bit interested. Back home in South Africa, things were not much different and I was told not to interfere when I saw some of the youngsters I had sold not performing as they should.

One of our yearlings that we sold had won the Guineas in the Free State and was coming to Cape Town for the Guineas here. As I knew the trainer very well, I begged to have a blood test done. When I read the blood I was horrified, as the horse was clearly incubating biliary or something very similar. I called the trainer up and said, 'I beg of you do not run on Saturday, your horse is sick (this was the Thursday) – it cannot win,' only to be informed that there was nothing wrong! I tried to explain that not only could it not win but that it would be ruined for good if it ran, but the trainer paid no attention to me. The horse did not win and never won another race. This happened on several occasions with horses that we had bred and even though I knew the trainers well, none of them paid the slightest bit of attention, so unsurprisingly I gave up trying.

* * *

Broadlands employed some wonderful people over the years. Before Hans Britz took over the stud we had various stud managers, one of whom was Mike Bass. He was a wonderful horseman and he left us to become a trainer. Today he is one of the most famous trainers in Africa, with world-famous horses under his belt, including possibly the greatest racehorse this country has ever produced – Pocket Power.

We had volunteers from all over the world coming to learn stud management, as Broadlands was quite famous by this time. For the many students who came here from England, Ireland, France and the United States it was a great opportunity to leave the northern hemisphere winter behind and to enjoy the African sunshine and lovely beaches down at Gordon's Bay.

When we started the stud, I managed to acquire the services of a wonderful veterinary surgeon, George Faull. He was my beloved vet for many years until tragically he died from cancer. I used to go and sit with him in the hospital; one feels so helpless watching such a great person gradually dying and knowing you can do absolutely nothing about it.

After George's death, I tried several other vets, but none of them could match his standards. Having spent so much of my time with Percy Sykes and George Faull and listening to them lecturing me on the various procedures, my expectations of a vet were understandably very high. I therefore decided to devise three tests of my own for any new vet I was thinking of employing, namely tubing, intravenous injections and follicle testing.

The first part was all to do with how the vet handled tubing. I had had a terrible experience when my lungs collapsed and a tube had to be inserted in such a rush that it tore part of my trachea, the result being that I was in agony every time I swallowed for ages after. I therefore surmised that horses would feel much the same way and so I always expected the vet to grease the tubing first and not to shove it down the horse's throat in a hurry.

My testing certainly screened out the majority. I found most vets lacked the gentle touch needed with the mares, many of them were in such a hurry either to get to the next appointment or to get home. Then the age-old issue of a demanding woman breathing down their neck resulted in many never returning. Finally I got word of a wonderful vet who had recently arrived from Rhodesia. He had been a show jumper and a very good horseman and his name was Jim Antrobus. He was quite simply brilliant and I often wondered if George Faull had intervened from his lofty abode to send me someone I could at last truly trust.

Whenever I was in Sydney, I would spend a lot of time each day at Percy's laboratory, studying haematology. He also gave me books he had written on the subject to take home and study. I have still proudly got a small green book that I think was his great breakthrough into racing haematology. What a difference his teaching was to make to my training methods – between Percy and Tommy, it was to utterly transform my life. I can never be sufficiently grateful to them for passing on to me their stupendous knowledge and for giving me some of the greatest years of my life. It was probably due to them that later on in my training career I was told that I was just one off a world record of 'Runners to Winners'.

CHAPTER

4

The first time I went to the Sydney Easter Sales I wanted to buy my mother six fillies and two colts. The extra fillies were with later breeding in mind. I studied my catalogue and marked only those with top pedigrees; another requisite was that they had to be by stallions who were proven getters of good fillies and thirdly – but most importantly – they had to have that certain something that separates a potentially great filly from an ordinary one. I paid no attention to advice from any of the agents or trainers – not even Tommy Smith! I knew that if Tommy fancied a yearling enough he would buy it for himself and if he was advising me, it was only because he thought the horse would do well in South Africa.

Mummy had been an enthusiastic gambler all her life and the buzz of a yearling sale was a bit like gambling, so she loved bidding. Having made my decisions I gave her my list and told her to bid and get the ones I had marked. I was coming from the yearling stables into the sales ring when just in front of me was a filly walking down the passageway to enter the ring. She was totally magnificent; she had a large, rather ugly head, but so bold, she looked at me as if she were Queen Boadicea. Her quarters were like a tank, her shoulders large yet straight and she had two rather straight front legs – but she had that certain something. I looked her in the eye and told her she was coming back with me, then I raced round to where Mummy was sitting – there was no time even to look her up in the catalogue to check her lineage. 'Mummy,' I said, 'there is a filly coming into the ring at any moment, I do not care how much she goes for, you just have to buy her.' Later I learnt she was by a stallion called Marazion and did not have much black type on the dam's side.

Mummy got her for $500 – the cheapest filly on the sale! I was so thrilled that I danced all the way down to her stable to kiss her on the nose. I named her after my adored mother – Miss Lindeman, my mother's maiden name. She turned out to be the South African champion sprinting filly and all sorts of stories surrounded her racing career. She even beat all the colts at weight-for-age in the Matchem Stakes over seven furlongs. Every time she ran she was simply unbeatable.

I bought another filly the following year at the same sales who was the total opposite to the *jolie laide* of Miss Lindeman. She was the perfection of beauty, a big black filly with a classically beautiful head with a white star, a swan-like neck and the most perfect body. Her only imperfection was she toed in, but front legs never bothered me as long as the filly spoke to me. She had big bold wonderful eyes and a lovely pedigree. Once again, Mummy received instructions to bid, which she happily did.

I named her Swan River, as when flying from South Africa to Australia, one's first stop is Perth, which is situated on the Swan River and is full of black swans. Back in South Africa, Swan River had trainers peering over the walls to see her. No one could fathom out why she was so fast and she became the most enchanting spoilt filly that ever raced. When transporting her I would bring along the geese and ducks who were her daily companions in her paddock and I also had all her favourite music played in her float.

It was at that same sale in Sydney that I also got Mummy to buy a filly for herself, Frank and Tubby Block. Tubby had told me he would like to go into partnership with Mummy in an Australian filly and this one seemed to be the perfect fit, with perfect pedigree and perfect conformation. She was not particularly beautiful, but she was without a doubt a perfect racing machine. I named her Miss International, as she was going to belong to three international owners. After the sale Tommy Smith, who had been the underbidder, came to me and told me he had wanted to buy the filly – but would Mummy consider letting him train her? I said that I was sure she would be delighted and I knew Frank would be too; I just had to ask Tubby, as I had already informed him of the purchase.

Tubby couldn't have been more pleased and so it was settled: Miss International went to Tommy. She won her first race in Australia very easily as a two-year-old, but tore all the ligaments in her back leg, so Percy Sykes suggested that as she would be very difficult to keep sound, Tommy should send her to me in South Africa. I had a marvellous track at Broadlands and this helped to heal her. I was so delighted to have her here and she did not disappoint, winning her first race in a canter and her second race by six lengths! A great fan of hers came to me after that race and said, 'Next time, please just ask your jockey to shake up the reins a little so that we can see just how far she can really win by,' which the fan thought could easily be 14 lengths.

Miss International won her next start again by half the race-track, but the tragedy was that she then got a bad case of biliary. Once she had recovered I gave her a six-month break, and then started training her again, but to my horror she collapsed on my track. I thought, as I raced down the track towards her, that she was dead, but Jim told me later that the biliary had affected her heart. He called up a man who worked with the famous sur-geon, Chris Barnard, and asked him what was the best procedure to keep Miss International going, as her heart was in such a bad way. The heart team came to the rescue and after examining Miss International, put her on a course of human heart medicines that worked wonders. She then retired to stud with the legacy of having been unbeaten in five races. Unsurprisingly and to my delight, all her progeny were black type.

The following year I asked Frank to buy Swan River's half-sister, who I named Rose Bay, and who became another champion, win-ning both the Cape and Durban Guineas. I also asked him to buy Marazion, the sire of Miss Lindeman. I had been to the stud to see him and so I knew he was going to be a real handful – a very big bay horse set to challenge all who came near him.

When Marazion was booked to fly back to South Africa, they had to remove him from the plane before take-off. In spite of the tranquillisers administered he had practically kicked the plane down. Eventually he came to South Africa by sea, together with a marvellous young Australian man called Paul as company. Having landed in Port Elizabeth he still needed to be transported to Cape Town – a trip he thanked me for by nearly taking my float apart.

Paul thankfully stayed with us on the farm for a while and helped settle the temperamental Marazion, which needless to say took some doing, but what a great stallion he turned out to be.

* * *

Another year had passed and my stables with the home-breeds and the Australian imports were full. When I built the racing stables, I designed them after the wonderful stables at Burrough Court, where I grew up. Those of course took 100 horses, compared to my mere 35 at a time!

The stables in England were built in a great square, which one entered under a huge archway with a clock tower on top. Mine, of course, were not nearly as grand; they were built in a square with a large plane tree in the middle on a grass lawn and just an ordinary archway, no clock towers. It was Tommy Smith's belief that all stables should be built so that the horses can see each other. The other requisite was that the colts had to be next to the fillies. The stables led out into huge paddocks for the race fillies and individual camps for the colts.

When she lived at Broadlands, Beryl Markham had built a track on the top part of the farm, but it was not ideal as it went uphill and downhill and there was no long stretch for sprinting. So the horses used to cross over the main road and go down to the beach to sprint. In those days the N2, although a main thoroughfare, did not have that much traffic and the section of Broadlands on the other side ran next to a lane that went down to the sea. Nowadays things are very different and the N2 is a major hazard, especially over the weekend when endless cars sit bumper to bumper as people make their way to and from Cape Town. The other side of the road, where once we walked the horses down to the beach, is now nothing but buildings. It is unrecognisable.

When I started training, I decided to move the racehorses to the lower farm. When Mummy bought Broadlands from the Kramers, this lower part of the farm was covered in vineyards and thankfully their son John had stayed on to help run this side of things. However, once John left we soon realised that none of us had a clue about the day-to-day running of a vineyard or indeed a wine farm – even though Mummy was a Lindeman!

So we pulled out the vines and under Tommy Smith's supervision we built an outstanding training track. Regular rides down at the beach were now not necessary, although we used to go once a week just to let the horses relax and do a bit of paddling in the surf. As we now had a lot of extra farmland available, at Tommy's suggestion I built extra paddocks for all the racehorses. The race fillies had two huge camps; we just used to remove their hind shoes after the races and they would all be turned out into the paddocks together. Having them moving about in the open paddocks helped to remove any build-up of lactic acid in their muscles which, as Percy Sykes used to point out to me, was a condition that race fillies were particularly prone to. Excessive lactic acid in a horse's muscles will cause it to tie up – this occurs when the muscles contract so severely that the horse cannot move. In addition to this and because of their high-protein diet, being left in a stable all day with only an hour's ride in the afternoon would result in them stiffening up. This way, after their morning meal, all the horses were turned out into the paddocks for the rest of the day. Here they were able to exercise all the time – the fillies would gallop around with their companions, graze on the grass, or eat oat hay and lucerne at their leisure. The colts had large individual camps, which were necessary as colts when put together will do nothing but fight with one another. At four o'clock they were all brought in for their evening meal and would then spend the night in their stables.

* * *

Broadlands as a stud farm was certainly taking off and so my annual trips to Australia now always coincided with the Easter Sales. Mummy would always join Frank and me – she used to rent a house in Rose Bay, where she then hired permanent maids to look after her, as there was not room for them in Frank's house. Her lady's maid, of course, travelled with her to attend to washing and ironing, the laying out of clothes and the running of baths and the like. Thankfully the very capable Shelagh, who was now living permanently at Broadlands, remained behind and took over the training of the horses while I was away.

After two or three years of buying yearlings at the Sydney Easter Sales – and now with our own thoroughbreds and my busy training schedules – it was not so easy to take time off to go to Australia. In addition to this I had reached capacity and did not need any new horses. Despite this, Mummy and Frank persuaded me to go for a month and this time Shelagh came too. We left the horses in the capable hands of a young man called Hans Britz – he had been a teenager living on Broadlands when we first bought the farm and was fast becoming an expert horseman. We armed Hans with a day-to-day schedule of the feed and the work programme for each horse and took off for Sydney.

I found a few lovely fillies on the sale and one evening as Shelagh and I were leaving the sale stables we saw a beautiful grey head hanging out over a stable door in noble curiosity. I had not yet looked at her, but soon found out she was a Sovereign Edition filly. We asked her groom to take her out of her box and she was pure perfection. Shelagh turned to me: 'We have got to get her!' she said. I had to agree. One thing all my fillies had to have was beautiful and bold eyes. This beauty not only had the eyes but a head to match. Talk about film star looks! In my estimation she was totally perfect and would have put the great Marilyn Monroe to shame.

When we checked in the catalogue we saw she had a pedigree to match her fine looks. So I wrote her number down and when the sales were on, instructed Mummy to buy her. I personally always preferred to look for that certain something – and to look at the catalogue after I had looked at the horses. Then hopefully they would be by a stallion that produced good fillies and had some good black type. However, failing this, if the filly still met my criteria, then the pedigree did not worry me. Unlike Miss Lindeman, this filly turned out to be the highest priced filly of the sale! I named her after my mother, whose last title had been Lady Kenmare, thus this new filly became Lady Kay, because she was, like my mother, so beautiful.

She also turned out to be an unbelievable race filly. She came second first time out and after that was unbeaten in 10 consecutive races. Then she retired to stud as I never raced my fillies beyond the age of four. Once they turned five they were sent up to the stud.

My Australian cousin, Rupert Fanning, who was about 11 years old at the time, often accompanied me to the sales and to Tommy Smith's gallops in the morning. Years later he told me that one morning, while we were watching Tommy Smith's two-year-olds going to the gallops, there was one particular filly that I fell in love with. Apparently I said to Rupert, 'Watch that filly – she's going to be a champion.' He then followed her racing career closely and she indeed went on to become Australia's champion filly. As a result of my influence, once he was old enough and able to do so, Rupert bought himself a racehorse. Now both he and his son have racehorses.

CHAPTER

5

Once we had become an established stud, I decided to design a modern medical room. We were buying so many fillies with the purpose of racing them and then putting them to stud – and horses are peculiar beings when it comes to mating. Covering mares is done just before the follicles ovulate and the mating season starts on 1 August until no later than the end of December each year. Running a stud farm requires a good amount of veterinary science along with a good amount of veterinary equipment.

I needed to design a new crush; this being a permanent structure built to restrain a horse while a veterinarian is examining her. I did not approve of the crushes being used in those days, which were made of solid iron with no quick exit for the horse should it panic. So I converted the old cattle barn into the medical room and designed my own crush, which consisted of one heavily padded wall about 1.3 metres high, then the other side a heavily padded swing gate of the same height. The reasoning behind this was that if at any time the mare panicked, the attending groom who was holding the gate could just swing it open and the mare could free herself. The rest of the room was a large area with the bottom half of the walls covered in designer yellow tiles, while the rest was painted white. On the walls I had lovely paintings of all our famous horses, which I added to as time went by. Also as time went by I started acquiring all my wild and exotic animals and soon the medical room looked like a Walt Disney fantasyland.

I laid a tarmac floor, with specially made rubber mats on top of this so that each day they could be taken out and hosed down with disinfectant. The foal always accompanied the mare and then the bottom of the stable door would be closed when they entered. I also put in a washbasin with a showerhead at the back of the crush where the vet stood, so the mare could be hosed down before and after examinations. In addition to this I installed a fridge and a glass cabinet in the same passageway and these were filled with all the necessary medicines and equipment. These included an ice machine, as we used to place ice down the boots of the horses to form an ice pack that was particularly good for healing any jarring of the horse's muscles.

Our new medical room was put together under the watchful eye of Jim Antrobus, who recently reminded me of the first time he came to the farm to do some work. I had been looking for someone brave enough to do a rectal examination on our very feisty mare Marysa. When George Faull was still alive he had tried to get her into the crush and she had practically destroyed the medical room along with the crush in protest. We never dared to try again but this meant that I had to guess when she might be ovulating and then put her in with a stallion and just hope for the best. This never worked so I persuaded Jim to try and examine her in her stable without the crush. I told him I would feed her some carrots and sugar cubes while he examined her. I was surprised when he agreed to this, as Marysa could easily have killed him, but to our joy, she stood quietly nibbling her treats while Jim did what he needed to do. From then on we never put her in a crush and I would distract her with titbits while Jim checked her ovaries. Jim reminded me that after the first successful examination he was invited up to the house for breakfast, wondering if the reason behind this was that since Marysa hadn't killed him he was now worth his weight in gold! It certainly worked out that way and we enjoyed many more subsequent breakfasts together over the years.

Jim told me how working at Broadlands had made him the vet he is today. In the early days, when money was never an issue, he had carte blanche to do whatever it took to save or heal a sick horse or foal. He would phone around the world and call on whoever he thought might be able to help. I was so pleased to hear that the work he did here has helped his career so much. Jim was behind us using lasers to assist with muscle tension in the horses. It was also amazing at removing haematomas. I got very proficient with the lasers and used to use the small laser on my friends' sore necks and backs with wonderful results. I also used it on myself.

* * *

The farm was fast becoming a large community of both people and animals. Hans's father was the night watchman for the stud. He was a very drunken old man, whom I often found early in the morning passed out in one of the mares' boxes. Using the anti-booze tablets common at the time I helped cure him of this awful habit. Hans, on the other hand, went from strength to strength. Beryl Markham had taught him how to ride, and when she left he had become one of my much-needed work riders. When he grew too tall, he became a groom in the racing stable and was the one entrusted with getting the racehorses safely to the races. When I started acquiring stallions for stud, I knew I would need a tall, competent horseman I could rely on to look after them and work under the stud manager. Hans was the obvious choice, and so he moved up to the stud section of the farm, where he soon became stud manager of Broadlands himself. Hans Britz made history as he was working here during the time of apartheid and it was unheard of at the time to have whites working under a coloured man – a notable feat for a young man of colour in those days.

One of the first 'wild animals' we had at Broadlands was Buster the baboon. Buster had been on the front page of the *Cape Argus,* Cape Town's leading morning paper. He was in need of rescuing and as I had had so much experience in Kenya with baboons, the SPCA was only too relieved to hand him over to my care.

Hans loved Buster and taught him to hold the mares' tails up while Jim Antrobus conducted his examinations. Jim would do what he needed to do, while Buster kept the tails held high, while the horse in question pressed in protest against the side of the crushes. Jim soon accepted this new type of groom as a useful assistant and not just a baboon.

Kalu, the chimpanzee who arrived in our lives a little later, was another story altogether. She adored Jim and would often make her appearance by climbing over the bottom part of the stable door, all the while hooting with delight while she leapt onto Jim's back. She would then wrap her great hairy arms around his neck and smother him in kisses. Jim took it all in his stride and continued to examine the mares while Kalu clung tight to his back.

Looking back, I sometimes wonder if Jim's present-day back issues are not connected to the great weight of Kalu hanging round his neck while he went quietly about his work with my horses. I used to sit beside Jim with my notebook, taking down all the follicle details and carefully noting when each mare was ready for covering. The only times when I did not enjoy this were when Jim picked up a twin on the ultrasound scan and had to carefully chase the little follicle around in order to pop it.

The floor wherever I sat busy with my note-taking was a sea of dogs, all beautifully behaved, lying at my feet like a beautiful carpet spread out around me. Every now and again my beloved cockatoo Molly would fly in and land on my shoulder. I do think the reason that all our resident mares, yearlings and foals were so calm and beautifully behaved was because they had been 'shock-proofed' by the menagerie at Broadlands. They had become accustomed to dogs running between their legs and monkeys grabbing their tails or riding them when they felt like it. One would often see the baby baboons in nappies clinging to the backs of the horses, who accepted these little riders with quiet stoicism. The brightly coloured wings of my cockatoo and macaws never startled the horses when descending to land on nearby fence posts.

While the horses may have been 'shock-proof', we were also being put through our paces when it came to being shocked. One of our very good work riders, Victor, who had been with us several years, was found one morning lying in the driveway – presumably dead. It was very early in the morning, and he was lying in the back drive, disembowelled, and the gravel from the road had been put into his stomach. We rushed him off to the hospital and the surgeons did an incredible job, so much so that a few months later he was back at work. We never did find out what he had done that might have elicited such an act of revenge. But whatever it was was clearly not forgotten, as two years later we found him decapitated on the main road below the farm.

Another violent episode on the farm occurred one year when I went to England. I had asked Shelagh if she would stay in the house while I was away, and thank goodness she had brought her friend Esme Flockerman to keep her company. Not long after we had left, Jim Antrobus was on the farm attending to some business when he noticed two ill-looking egrets in the paddocks – he thought they might have botulism and was therefore worried about the horses. The questionable birds were caught, placed in a cardboard box and left in the scullery. Later that evening Shelagh had a look at them, decided they weren't ill at all, and opened the back door to put them out. The dogs were making an awful noise and as she was putting the birds out the first bird fell off the back of the kitchen wall. She was going to step down to look at the bird when something did not feel right and she quickly closed the back door. Going round to the dining room door she peered through the glass pane to see what the dogs were on about and here she encountered the first of the three men, his face pressed up against the other side of the glass with the barrel of a gun pressed up against the other pane.

Shelagh quickly took flight down the passage with the sound of breaking glass not far behind her. Deciding that the safest place was definitely outside, she ran through into Esme's room, slammed the bedroom door after her and then out through the French doors that led onto the pool area, all the while shouting for Esme to follow. Meanwhile, Esme, on hearing all the noise, had loaded her own gun and quickly followed Shelagh outside. Esme's bedroom door was hard to open, as it was swollen from recent rain and this slowed the men down significantly, giving her time to position herself behind one of the pillars by the pool. The men, for reasons unknown to anyone at the time, shot several bullets about her room (to this day I have kept one of the bullets lodged in the beautiful Elizabethan-style four-poster bed). In the meantime, Shelagh had hidden behind the pool pump house. With great bravery, Esme started shooting at the robbers, one of whom was so terrified he also ran and hid, and in so doing ended up next to Shelagh. She said they were jammed together in the small space and he was shaking with fright. His two companions raced away to escape the hail of bullets from Esme's gun and he also then took off when he saw them disappearing. The police told us later that the man doing the shooting had not used a gun before, which explained why he shot the bed post and a number of other random holes fairly high up in the room – apparently the kick back from his gun had on each occasion taken him by surprise, leaving him unable to aim in any one direction. Esme had known at the time that she had cancer, and Shelagh says she was delighted to have had the chance to fire her gun before she died, which she did not long after this incident.

Another stressful situation Shelagh had to endure when I was away was looking after Mummy – this time I was on my yearly visit to my beloved house at Karen. Mummy had not wanted to go; she was very happily ensconced at Broadlands, but I could not leave her on her own, so asked Shelagh to stay with her and in particular to accompany her when she was driving and not to let her drive too fast, if possible. Mummy never obeyed the rules of the road and was very reckless, having no fear whatsoever; she drove like an absolute lunatic. All her chauffeurs had resigned because they were never allowed to drive and were kept in the back seat cowering in terror at every turn. That is why I never allowed her to drive when I was with her and had constituted myself her chauffeur. She had one poor bridge friend who ended up with shingles, she said as a result of having to accompany my mother on her bridge outings.

Shelagh, who is a good driver, managed to drive Mummy most of the time I was away, therefore giving her the opportunity to play with her hyrax and meerkat, which she used to have on leads as they would accompany her everywhere, usually draped around her neck. However there were a few occasions when Mummy insisted on taking the wheel, and they have never been forgotten by poor Shelagh!

Shelagh soon became my assistant trainer, in charge of the stable management and feeding. As the feeding followed a strict Percy Sykes diet, this was practically a full-time job on its own, as the additive to increase the protein of toasted soya bean had to be carefully measured in a special mug. In addition to this, each horse had to have so many scoops of whole oats, so many mealies, so much bran and molasses – and some of the horses, according to their blood reading, needed more of this or that than the others. Percy had said never to give crushed oats, as the crushing took all the goodness (protein) out of the oats. Percy analysed everything: he used to get me to run around collecting horse manure for him so that he could analyse that as well.

CHAPTER

6

When we first moved from Kenya to Broadlands, amongst the horses that we brought from Kenya was an English mare called Xylone. She was the dam of Kenya's champion racehorse, Lone Eagle, who Beryl had named after Charles Lindbergh, the first man to fly the Atlantic – Lone Eagle being the nickname an adoring public gave him.

Xylone won the Kenya Derby and she continued to win in South Africa. Once she finished racing she was put to stud, and at one time we had as many as 18 of her daughters and granddaughters with their foals on Broadlands. What a champion brood mare Xylone turned out to be; her progeny have won innumerable Grade 1 races in South Africa.

The Durban July is South Africa's major race day. Everyone gets dressed up – though the young women seem to interpret that as under-dressing, showing lots of flesh and revelling in wearing minuscule pieces of transparent fabric, while their escorts don weird and wonderful colours to complement their female companions. All of this adds to and forms part of the big day.

At the Durban July in 2008 there were four Grade 1 races, one of which was the Golden Horseshoe for juvenile colts, which was won by Forest Path, a direct descendant of my wonderful Xylone. Another Grade 1 race that day was won by a filly called Outcome, a direct descendant of my glorious Australian mare Bejewel. Then the two Garden Province Grade 1 races for fillies and mares were won by horses that were from the sire lines of my two champion brood mare sires, Royal Prerogative and Averof.

At the Durban July the following year, in 2009, the July itself was won by a South African champion three-year-old, Big City Life, a descendant of Royal Prerogative. The third horse home was Forest Path, who had done so well the previous year. Forest Path, in addition to being the grandson of Xylone, was also a descendant of Royal Prerogative. One of the Grade 1 races of the day was won by another great filly, Lady Windemere, who was also a descendant of Royal Prerogative. So those amazing sires of Broadlands are still producing champion descendants today – what a pleasure it is to see.

My great friend John Freeman, who is a steward of the Jockey Club and a famous bloodstock agent, said to me, 'Bringing in those two stallions Royal Prerogative from England and Averof from Australia has been one of the highlights of the South African breeding industry.'

Xylone died at the ripe old age of 32, in the Broadlands racing stables. I used to let her wander around loose in the daytime as she was such an elderly lady. When she used to come into her stable at night, she would walk peacefully through all the rescued geese and ducks, have a good meal and put herself to bed. Shelagh always saw that she had extra titbits of carrots and apples cut up for her, which she loved. This day it was about 3pm when she came into the stable yard and lay down under the plane tree in the middle of the yard. She closed her eyes and we thought she had gone to sleep, but when evening came and she had not moved, we realised she had died.

This wonderful old lady who had had such an effect on South African racing, travelling half-way around the world from England to Kenya and South Africa, had ended her long life in the shade of a plane tree.

* * *

The first of the great fillies I trained were from my visit to the Australian yearling sales in 1971 and 1972 – they were Miss Lindeman and Swan River. Two more different looking fillies it would be hard to find. Swan River, when I took her out of her stable to have a look at her, was quite the most beautiful filly one could ever hope to see, totally feminine, tall and black with the most beautiful classical head and a magnificent body – although Terrance Millard, one of South Africa's great world-class trainers, once told me he thought she would never race as she toed in so badly. He had come out to Broadlands one day to look over my Australian imports and I clearly remember him turning to me and saying, 'Why did you buy her? She will never see the racecourse.' Terrance had a thing about good front legs, but it never worried me, as long as they had what it takes – and Swan River had it.

Miss Lindeman, by contrast, was a huge, rather masculine filly, rather ugly (although not to me – I thought she was quite beautiful). When she was in serious training and about to have her first race, Sir Cecil Charles Boyd-Rochfort and his wife, who were great friends of my mother's, came to stay. Sir Cecil would lean heavily on 'his walking stick as my string walked by, observing them all intently. One day he picked up his stick to point at Miss Lindeman and said, 'Let me have a look at that filly.' He studied her carefully, pointed out her faults and said, 'If she does not break down she will be a champion.' He was right, none of her faults stopped her from becoming a champion South African filly. She was a six-furlong specialist, which in today's racing distances is 1 207 metres, although the only time I ran her over seven furlongs, in the Matchem Stakes, she won that as well.

I had a strategy when I started training my new babies: the ones that showed real promise, either on my track or when I took them for gallops on the racecourse, were never allowed to be beaten in training. Their working companion, always an older horse and a top division gelding, would have to hold back in order to make sure that they always got their head in front at the winning post. I found with fillies and the few colts I trained that if they got a feel, from an early age, of what it meant to win, they never let anyone ahead of them. This certainly worked with Miss Lindeman – and later, perhaps to a detrimental effect, with the infamous filly Marysa.

When Miss Lindeman went for her first race, Mummy and everyone backed her, she hit the front just before the winning post and then shied to the right, which cost her the race. It seemed that she had taken fright at the shadow formed across the track by the winning post and her jockey confirmed this. A few days after the race, I went to see Mrs Van again. I was worried about my mother's health and wanted to know if there was anything I could do to help. I was not thinking about the horses, when Mrs Van said to me, 'I have got a message for you from my guide, he says that you have a horse with a big white face' – clearly this referred to Miss Lindeman's blaze. She then continued, 'I do not understand what he is saying, but he seems to be indicating that you must close the eyes and then it will never stop winning.' Mrs Van then took her hands and closed them over her eyes. She was obviously indicating that Miss Lindeman needed blinkers, despite her lack of racing knowledge. I immediately had a pair made for her in my mother's racing colours (I still have them to this day) and next time she ran, thanks to Mrs Van, there was simply no stopping her.

Once I started to work on Swan River to get her ready to race, I could not believe what I was seeing – she just needed work, work and more work. She became the South African champion staying filly, winning The Oaks and beating all the colts in the Lonsdale Stirrup Cup as a three-year-old, before going to Durban to win the second Oaks of her career. No filly had ever arrived in Durban with such a high race figure, and a filly beating colts was unheard of at this time. In her two seasons of racing, she was to become famous throughout South Africa and win me 10 races in total. She was placed eight times; in fact, out of all of her starts, she was only unplaced once.

The day I took her for her first grass gallop at Kenilworth, she paralysed the competition, so I thought, 'I'll teach you, you little madam!' The next time, I took two top division horses with her. It was a six-furlong gallop on the Kenilworth grass and my instructions to my work riders not to let her be beaten were totally unnecessary – in the last furlong she passed them all as if they did not exist, and came back totally full of herself, hardly blowing and prancing about like a ballet dancer.

I could almost swear that, as she was being unsaddled, she looked me in the eye and winked. 'See, you idiot,' she was saying to me, 'I am not one of your usual horses – I am a bloody champion.' Anyhow, I gave her kisses and a special treat of lump sugars, and whispered in her ear, 'I have a feeling you are probably right.' She certainly was.

First race day dawned and I had announced confidently to the press that she was unbeatable, so she started as favourite. The racing crowd craned forwards to get a glimpse of the beautiful film star cantering down to the start. It was a memorable occasion, but then what was even more memorable was that she held up the whole start as she refused to go into the gates and had to be withdrawn. The race went off without the star attraction, who came cantering back pleased as punch with herself.

I called up Tommy Smith for a solution to the problem. He told me to get my own starting gates and tranquillise her, then steadily reduce the dose as she got used to standing and going into the stalls. I did this and used to give her sugar cube treats as she stood there, beautifully well behaved. On race day I went down with her to the start and was about to give her sugar cubes when the stipe stopped me in my tracks: 'Strictly not allowed,' he said. In hindsight I suppose he thought I was about to give her some form of performance-enhancing drug.

Then the race began, and as predicted my beautiful film star came away from the field in the last furlong, not even bothering to raise a hard gallop and she practically cantered past the winning post, about six lengths clear! In the winner's enclosure, my angel was not even blowing and looked at me as if to say, 'Give me something a bit harder next time – that was a piece of cake.' I could tell she loved being the star attraction.

I have trained many fillies in my time, but Swan River seemed to know that she was the most beautiful of them all. She constantly acted like a prima donna, almost saying to the crowds as she came into the winner's enclosure, 'Take a good look; you will never see the likes of me again.'

As she raced she became more and more famous. The Africans in the crowd adored her and would applaud as she came into the ring; in response she would dance around with a groom on either side. The grooms would be dressed in blue, the Broadlands colours, with blue and white knitted caps on their heads, and to match Swan River sported a white bridle imported especially from Australia, with a blue and white browband. Her mane was always neatly plaited to show off that glorious swan-like neck and her rich black coat when caught in the sunlight showed off the brushed quarter marks on her magnificent quarters. To finish the picture the top of her tail was plaited. She stood out like a Botticelli painting.

In those days no other trainers or owners paid that much attention to the groom's outfit or to the enhancement of the beauty of their horses. I like to think I was a leader in the field in this regard, although in truth I know all the other trainers thought I was as mad as a hatter. But I loved Swan River to bits and she knew it well! She was spoilt rotten by Shelagh, all my staff and myself and as she worked her way up to the top of the fillies' tree with her wonderful racing exploits, she became more and more spoilt and more and more demanding!

Music had to be played to her in the float when she was travelling to the races and on any long journeys – this we did with an old battery-powered transistor radio – so she became au fait with the top of the pops. In addition to this she had to be accompanied by her lead pony and all her favourite chickens (which I had rescued over the years). She refused to eat with her head in the manger unless it was hooked to the outside of her door, so that she could lean out and keep an eye on all her clucking and crowing friends below as she ate. Shelagh was the only person I entrusted with driving her float and she told me that whenever they stopped to fill up with petrol on the way to Durban for the season, the forecourt staff would rush up to the float when they learnt that their heroine Swan River was inside. This was the early seventies, when racing was the only form of legal gambling in the country and consequently was a major source of income.

Swan River only raced as a three- and four-year-old. She was so brilliant that she won all distances from five furlongs to 12 furlongs, which in today's terms would be 1 000 to 2 400 metres. Before her staying races – which were, as the term implies, longer distances of 1 600 metres or over – I would let her win a local six-furlong sprint, which is what I did before I took her to Durban, for The Oaks. This was going to be her first visit to Durban, as well as mine.

Her blood readings, which I was constantly monitoring, told me that she was still not fit enough, so I wanted to give her another hard race, even though she had had her sprint. I entered her for the mile and a half Lonsdale Stirrup Cup at Kenilworth in Cape Town. She was the only filly in the race and everyone advised me against it, saying I was asking the impossible, especially with The Oaks ahead of her. I asked Shelagh and Frank what they thought and they both agreed that with the way she was running she had a very good chance of winning. So I then went and had a conversation with my beautiful Swan River, telling her of my intention, and she seemed to be perfectly happy to go along with my plan, giving little soft whinnies into my ear as I was kissing her. So the Lonsdale Stirrup Cup day dawned and the brilliant South African jockey,

Garth Puller, who was riding her, told me he wanted to be in the first five as they came round the last bend. Garth rode her to perfection, as usual, and she romped home beating all the colts. I was so proud of her as she danced her way off for a blood test to check she had been given no performance-enhancing drugs, all the while looking as if she had not even had a morning gallop.

A wonderful piece of news that came through the same day was that her dam, Sahiba, and half-sister Rose Bay (another champion to be) had finally docked in Cape Town from Australia.

The next big hurdle in Swan River's life was to be The Oaks. I had booked a room at the Cabana Beach Hotel just outside Durban. Here I had special permission to bring my two Great Danes and Frank and I settled into a lovely suite on the ground floor. We were given two stables at Clairwood in Eileen Bestel's yard. She was a famous trainer in Durban and had some very good racehorses. She became one of my greatest friends and put up with the very spoilt Swan River upsetting her immaculately run stable yard – as it now had to host the companion ducks and chickens. In addition to this, a small paddock had to be built off her stable so that Swan River could have her hours of freedom accompanied by her lead horse. And then, of course, there was the music that had to be played to her so that she could relax in the comfort of her stable.

Swan River's fame had preceded her; no three-year-old filly had ever come to The Oaks with such a high race figure. The following morning her rider, a lead horse on one side and a groom hanging onto the other side, accompanied her to her early-morning gallops. As usual it took three people and an accompanying horse to get her safely to the track in the mornings. She was always cavorting about like a ballerina and was so fresh and full of herself that I was always in a state, in case she got loose and hurt herself. This scene occurred daily and I was always following nervously behind on foot, prepared to pick up the pieces.

Being an incredible beauty, and with her entourage all dressed in the sky blue of the Broadlands stable colours, along with her Australian pale blue quarter sheet with its large fringes, swaying about with all the prancing about – she looked quite simply exquisite!

I had wanted Garth Puller, who was familiar with Swan River, to come to Durban for this race, but unfortunately he couldn't make it. However, I was lucky enough to get hold of a champion South African jockey called Johnny Cawcutt. I asked Johnny if he would work ride Swan River for a few days before the race, so he could get to know her, as he was often at Clairwood in the mornings. I told him that I would like him to first trot for a mile and a half and then work her hard from a mile and a half, and finally to sprint the last five furlongs. Despite my instructions, he seemed to slow all her work down and when she returned to the stables she was a bit like a ticking time bomb ready to explode. Not wanting to hurt his feelings, I waited until he had left, then put my work rider on her and repeated the performance. This was the order of events we then followed for the next few days leading up to race day. The rumours about this amazing Australian filly and her crazy trainer were rife, with Johnny her jockey apparently telling people that he thought that if I continued to work her like this she would be dead by race day.

The evening before The Oaks I asked Brian Baker, a brilliant Durban-based vet, to come and drench Swan River, as I wanted to replace all the bodily fluids lost through sweating. I only realised afterwards that other trainers had never seen all the modern developments I had been exposed to, and as I had never trained from public stables, even more rumours started flying around, including how I was administering worm medicine the evening before the race. All this talking and gossiping resulted in a public conclusion that there was no way that she could win, so from favourite she went clean out of the betting.

The day before the race Shelagh had to fly up from Cape Town. I just did not trust anybody else to drive my beloved Swan River all the way to the Greyville racecourse and to saddle and bridle her for the race. Despite all my years of experience with horses, I had never actually learned to saddle or fit a bridle properly, as there had always been vast numbers of grooms to prepare my ponies, hunters and steeplechasers. So when it came to the practical side of things, I was incompetent as ever; it made sense that Shelagh, who was very competent, could do all the niceties of preparing the horses on race day.

Swan River's jockey, Johnny Cawcutt, raced in my husband Frank's colours, as she was the one I had chosen for him at the Sydney sale. So there she was, bedecked in scarlet and orange that looked very good set against her beautiful black coat. My nerves were in knots and I spent my time hiding in the toilets praying for her. I also asked my beloved friend Father Tom, a Catholic priest and great racing enthusiast, to pray for her, as he had come up to see her run. When at the Cape races, Father Tom used to stand by the winning post to help my horses return safely with his blessing. I was always so frightened that some harm might come to them, as there are horrific racing accidents at times.

We enjoyed a very good lunch in the restaurant with all our friends who had come to support the famous Swan River, then settled into the stands for the race. I had told Frank that according to the blood results from the day before, she could not lose, and I could certainly not see another filly in sight with the form to beat her. There may well have been great fillies there that day, but Swan

River was quite simply a superstar. Frank, when I gave him the go-ahead, loved placing a bet and as she was returning a good price due to her lost popularity, he had put a lot on her.

She looked so gorgeous on the way up to the start that it brought tears to my eyes; whether she won or lost she was still the most beautiful filly I had ever encountered. Johnny Cawcutt was not champion jockey for nothing, and I knew he had the ability to give her a superb ride. I told him that she must come from behind and be given time to settle and then it was all up to him. As soon as the gates opened he did just that and she was lying about fifth. Then as they came to the final bend and straightened up for the home run, he just let her go and within seconds she had cruised past the finish line well ahead of any competition. We all made a mad exodus to the winning box where we smothered her in kisses and pats – she knew only too well that she was the star of the show, as usual!

The next day she appeared to be in such fine form that I decided to give her one more run before returning to the Cape, so we entered her into the Natalia Stakes, another feature race, two weeks later. This time she was a hot favourite and her looks and reputation clearly had an effect on the Durban race crowds who cheered for her loudly as she appeared in the paddock before the race, and then gave her a wildly enthusiastic ovation as she returned to the paddock after winning the race.

The following year we took her back to Durban as a four-year-old and she won the Natalia Stakes once again before retiring to stud, where she became a champion brood mare.

That year, Frank and I stayed at the Umhlanga Rocks Hotel, where we once again shared a lovely ground floor apartment with the Great Danes – with a lawn in front overlooking the rocks, beyond which was a winding path to the beach below. Through racing, I had made great friends with a lovely Indian family called the

Chettys and we used to enjoy wonderful curry dinners with them whenever we were near Durban. Following this, we often went to the Indian cinemas – not that I was that keen on Indian movies, as no matter how beautiful they were, they used to last for about three hours!

We could not invite the Chettys to the Umhlanga Rocks Hotel as these were the terrible days of apartheid. This seemed so strange to me, as Mummy, Rory and I had spent so many magical days and nights in India and had received such wonderful hospitality when we were there. I had ridden all over India from the Himalayas to the very south – in fact, the early-morning gallops for some of India's top trainers in what was then Bombay and is today Mumbai, are some of my finest memories.

One year, the Chettys took me to the Indian market in Durban. Indian people have a wonderful eye for colour, materials and craftsmanship and even the display of vegetables seemed to have taken on a special exotic beauty. Walking through the market I was in a dream-world filled with colour and scent, until I turned a corner and stopped in my tracks. There before me were two truly magnificent scarlet macaws cramped into a tiny little cage that was surrounded by a group of horrible children who were poking sticks at them. Thank goodness they were for sale, so I bought them on the spot and went straight to the nearest pet shop to buy them big enough cages until I could get them home.

Frank would sit in his swimming shorts on the grass in the mornings at the Umhlanga Rocks, drying out after his early-morning swim, and he would take the macaws to sit beside him while I was busy at the track. The first morning this happened he knew he was onto a good thing, as he said to me later: 'If only I'd thought up this gimmick before I remarried you! I've had a swarm of lovely girls all coming over to admire the bloody birds and had it not been for you, I could have been chatting the lot of them up!' Although I suspect this did not on any account stop him.

Poor Frank, having been so famous in Australia as a great swimming champion, bedecked with gold medals, had become used to being followed around by a bevy of female groupies from which he could take his pick. Now all he had to rely on were these bright-feathered birds for constant company!

Our stay at the Umhlanga Rocks Hotel with the Great Danes was very funny, as they slept on the bed with us at night and since the bed in the hotel was not as big as our special bed at home, each night resulted in an animal and human sprint to secure the best spot. One night, after having come a poor fourth in the bed race, I had to laugh: 'At our age, here we are trying to outrun the dogs so that we can get ourselves comfortably settled for the night, while there is still some space left,' I said to Frank. 'If anyone could see us they would be convinced that we were insane.'

Soon after Swan River won the Natalia Stakes, we returned to the Cape. This time Swan River was accompanied on the return journey by the two macaws from the market as well as her chickens and geese. The macaws later became a great feature at Broadlands, as once they were acclimatised I let them loose to fly about as they pleased.

On subsequent trips to Durban we used to go to the Oyster Box Hotel, as the Umhlanga Rocks was sold. Here we had our own bungalow. It was perfectly lovely as the vervet monkeys used to come and sit on our roof, making me feel right at home. Such an amusing incident happened there; I had to spend a lot of time at Greyville for a few days as I had a filly running, but Frank was in great pain at the time with gout, which I kept telling him was from celebrating with too much champagne. He could hardly move, so I asked his sister Betty to come and look after him while I was gone.

Betty had at this point been living at Broadlands and operating a thriving retail business of imported Indian materials. While we had arranged a guest suite for Betty, she chose instead to move into the spare bed in our bungalow – this made perfect sense of course as she was then closer to Frank and better able to care for him. On the second day, I got a call from the very nice receptionist at the Oyster Box: 'Mrs O'Neill, I don't know how to tell you this, but I think you had better come back; there is a lady that has moved into your room with your husband.' I thanked her very much for the information, but did explain that it was in fact his sister. This sort of attentive customer service is practically non-existent today.

These trips to Durban we made with Swan River were so memorable as she only had two seasons of racing. Her racing life was immensely successful except for one disaster, when like an idiot I decided to take her to Johannesburg for the Holiday Inn, one of the biggest staying races in the country at the time. Today the race is no longer sponsored by the Holiday Inn and is known as the Summer Cup over 2 000 metres.

Johannesburg is 6 000 feet above sea level and I had not taken this fact into consideration. This was strange, as in Kenya I lived at very high altitudes and was so accustomed to it – I should have remembered how in my young days in Mexico City I used to get so breathless when I was dancing. Swan River was flown up on the day of the race and there was therefore no time to take a blood reading, which had been perfect before she left.

Poor, dedicated, wonderful Shelagh flew up with Swan River on the morning of the race; Garth Puller was riding her as he knew her so well and everything seemed to be going well. Swan River always liked to come from behind, but for some strange reason Garth took her to the front when they reached the top of the incline for the last bend. She must have been at least five lengths clear of the competition, when she suddenly packed up. After the race I had never seen her so distressed. She was blowing so badly, she could hardly breathe – and this from a filly that used to come away from her races as if she was ready to start all over again!

This was to be her second-last race. I firmly decided to keep away from the Johannesburg altitude and took her to Durban for the Natalia Stakes, where she could end her racing life on a high note with a clean win – which she did.

Then her second round of success began, and my joy reached new heights when she went to stud. With the combination of her and my wonderful stallion Royal Prerogative, she became a champion brood mare. From the moment she went to stud, practically every foal she bred was black type. One of her greatest sons, Swan Prince, won the Champion Stakes, a big feature race in Johannesburg, ridden by the hero of English racing, the great Lester Piggott.

CHAPTER

7

When I first saw Swan River turning out to be such a champion, I called up Frank, who was in Australia at the time, and asked him to buy her dam, Sahiba. He asked Bob Young, owner of Australia's biggest racehorse transport company, and a long-time friend, to go to the stud and arrange the deal for him. When Bob got there, he called up Frank to tell him there was also a yearling filly going – Swan River's half-sister. I begged Frank to buy her, which he then did, along with Sahiba and a stallion called Istanbul – why I do not know, as he was not young at the time and did not turn out to be much good. This was not to say that Frank didn't have a good eye for a champion stallion, as it was Frank who bought the brilliant Averof.

While they were awaiting transport to South Africa, Bob arranged for the filly to go to a well-known handler of yearlings. After a couple of weeks the handler called up and said. 'You can't let these friends of yours keep this filly, she is stone crazy! When you want to do anything with her, if she is not trying to kill you against the wall of the stable, she is throwing herself on the floor. The only answer to this problem is a bullet in the brain.' We all chose to ignore these dire warnings – and not long after this the ship docked in Cape Town with my future champion filly aboard.

Frank went down to meet them and see the new arrivals. He said to Bob, who had accompanied the horses on their journey, 'The filly Swan River is running in a big race this afternoon – the Lonsdale Stirrup Cup. Pat also has another horse running called Mexican Summer; both horses will win, so give me some money and I will back them both for you.' Bob, along with the entire ship, from the captain downwards, all quickly handed their bets over to Frank. That night there were terrific celebrations aboard the ship, as both horses had duly won and everybody was a lot richer as a result.

Chris Barnard, who had become a great racing enthusiast of my stables, had also won a fair bit that day. Unable to go to the shipboard celebrations himself, he suggested that some of his nursing staff would love to take part. So when Frank arrived with all his friends and some of the glamorous nurses, he was the hero of the ship's crew.

Meanwhile, our new arrivals were being settled at Broadlands and I decided to name our feisty new filly Rose Bay. This was because my Uncle Grant had a lovely house on the water's edge in Rose Bay in Sydney, with a garden going right down to the sea. I often used to stay there and had such wonderful memories of his home. As predicted, she did throw herself around a few times, but she soon sorted herself out and became another spoilt pet just like her half-sister Swan River, eating handfuls of sugar cubes from my hands. When Bob later told his friend, the handler who had broken her in, that she had gone on to become a champion race filly he just shook his head in disbelief.

I had been so excited to lay eyes on Rose Bay, though she looked no more like Swan River's half-sister than the man in the moon. She could indeed have come from a different planet. She was a big bay with a strong white blaze and a bold, but not particularly lovely head. She did have great big quarters and lovely shoulders. I was utterly thrilled and soon realised that I had another champion on my hands. We were in the stable yard one day when Frank came over with his great pal from next door, Gurd van Heesch, who had become an ardent racing fan; he was a big gambler and had won a considerable amount of money on my marvellous race fillies.

Frank was keen to show him our new star on the horizon. I had brought Rose Bay out into the yard, when I heard Gurd saying to Frank, 'I would like to buy her from you.' Frank then told him she was not for sale. Next thing, to my utter horror, Gurd said, 'I will toss you for her,' and Frank said 'OK' – I could have bloody killed him! Frank, of course, lost the toss, but I said to them both, 'I could not care how much honour is involved; there is no way she is leaving my stable.' Frank, however, was the official owner of Rose Bay, so with not much leg room, I simply told them that she would stay with me and I would train her.

So Rose Bay became Gurd's first racehorse. All because of a silly old tossed coin!

Rose Bay did not require anywhere near the amount of work her sister did; the only thing they had in common was their idiosyncrasies. As my racing stables were built in such a way that all the horses could see each other, I chose to put her next to a magnificent little colt called Mexican Summer. I had put Mexican Summer on the yearling sales that year, but he was so small that nobody wanted him, so thank heavens he did not reach his reserve price. Happily, I kept him and despite his small size, he turned out to be a champion sprinter, winning me 11 races as well as performing the part of 'toy boy' to the very spoilt Rose Bay.

Mexican Summer was black – I have stalwartly refused to call any horse I have ever owned brown, although today black horses are now called dark bay. Despite being only 14.2 hands, whereas most colts of that age are about 16 hands, he was very determined and would just keep poking that lovely little black nose of his out in front, just before the winning post – it was a remarkable scene, time and time again! I remember when he was just a foal and kept getting under the paddock fences to play with the dogs; he and the Great Danes were about the same size and enjoyed a good run about together.

Swan River had to be accompanied by various animals, but all Rose Bay needed was her constant companion – Mexican Summer. She was so besotted with him that she refused to roll in the sand ring after her morning workouts unless he had his head hanging over the side nickering at her. I also used him as her working companion, so of course he had to accompany her to Durban, work on the track with her in the mornings and be in the little paddock next to hers during the day. The racing public often used to come and watch this famous twosome – and when Mexican Summer won his races, needless to say Rose Bay was by his side.

I was grateful throughout my racing career that I had learned about haematology from Percy Sykes, the world master of racehorse blood analysis – and never more so than when it came to Mexican Summer, who haemoconcentrated very badly. This resulted in increased blood viscosity, so I always had to drip him before his races to thin his blood. If we hadn't done this, he would probably never have won more than one or two races, instead of the magnificent 11 he went on to win.

Finally I had to retire him, as his handicap kept increasing: the more he won, the more weights they kept plonking onto his small back. In the end I could not bear to see my lovely little boy struggling so hard to make it to the front where he knew he belonged.

Rose Bay won a Cape Town Fillies Guineas, and after this I took her to the Natal Fillies Guineas, which she also won. In addition to this, she had won her three races prior to the Guineas, but I could only race her very sparingly, as every time she came back after a race, she was very lame behind and had to live on MSM – a natural compound derived from the bark of trees. This was due to the concussion in the legs from hard pounding on the grass tracks as they raced. I used to use a combination of MSM and laser treatment for several months at a time, but this soon became too much for both of us and so I decided to retire her to stud early.

Gurd, the neighbour and owner, made a killing. From the 10 starts during her racing career, Rose Bay placed five and won five – unbelievably good statistics for a young filly. When she retired to stud she was a champion brood mare; amongst other champions she bred was the great Mark Anthony, by Royal Prerogative. Mark Anthony became a legendary winner in South Africa.

* * *

Bob Young, who lived in Melbourne, used to accompany many of my yearlings on their sea voyages from Australia and had some horrific resultant tales to tell. The first lot he brought over – Bejewel, Young Susan, Lady Kay and Australia Fair – endured three days of terrible storms out in the Indian Ocean, with the waves crashing over the horse boxes and drenching the horses. Lady Kay got badly cast, and Bob struggled to get her back on her feet again. It was just downright amazing that none of the others got hurt. Bob recalled that getting them all cleaned up and getting dry bedding to them was a tremendous task, as he could hardly stand upright and had to keep rushing to the side of the ship to be sick.

A similar scene took place the following year when he brought a number of new yearlings, including Rose Bay, as well as Sahiba and the stallion Istanbul. This time the weather was simply horrendous. The horse boxes received the full force of the ocean and Bob was not allowed to go down to them for two days in case he got swept overboard. When the captain finally let him down, he descended with dread as to what he might find. Not having been able to give them food or water for all of this time, he could not believe his eyes when he found them alive and unhurt.

Bob has a lovely 'rags to riches' life story. He was born in Melbourne into a very impoverished family, who were given shelter in old army barracks. He was one of about nine siblings. Often their mother was only able to give them soup, which would have to last them for three days, so to help out, from the age of eight he used to sell newspapers on the street corner and then proudly bring home the five or six shillings he had made, which he would give to his mother. When he was 18 he had to do compulsory military training; he loved life in the army and became a warrant officer 1st class. There he met Allen Reeves, the son-in-law of Jack Garret, who owned the largest horse racing transport business in Australia. He was offered a job with the company and there he remained for 40 years, as their most trusted and sought-after driver.

After 35 years he bought the company but still kept on driving, then after another 10 years he sold the company and retired. He has a wonderful wife, two very successful sons and a daughter. He adores his family and in 2000 they all clubbed together and the whole family went on a first-class world tour to England and Europe. Bob chose to come and spend two weeks with us while the family were in Crete and it was just so lovely having him here at Broadlands again after so many years, in spite of having to listen every day to what a wonderful family he had! He also had so many great racing stories to tell and never stopped helping around the farm. What a wonderful generous person he is.

* * *

The few colts that I did buy over the years at the Sydney sales were hugely successful – but once they started winning all the two-year-old races the Jockey Club put a ban on them racing in Juvenile races, or even the lesser handicaps. Then they established a new rule altogether: Australian colts now had to start in the B Division. That put a swift stop to the importation of colts – the Jockey Club had certainly made their point! However I was unfazed by a ruling that was clearly directed at me, as I now had a number of wonderful homebred fillies that were starting to set the tracks alight. Apart from my brilliant little colt Mexican Summer, I concentrated on breeding and training fillies and used to sell the colts, unless of course they did not meet their reserve; then I kept them and trained them myself.

Some of the colts, despite my better judgement, surprised me no end. Highborn Harry was born in 1976 and came from my brilliant little mare Naughty Nymph. He was a magnificent chestnut and looked just like his sire, Royal Prerogative. Not meeting his reserve price at the sales, I took him home, where I started training him and very soon I could not believe what I was seeing. He was living dynamite on my gallops and when I took him to the track he sailed past all the top division older horses. I had another champion! Before his first race I informed the press that he could not be beaten. Because of this, I believe he started at the shortest odds ever known for an unraced two-year-old in South Africa, and he went on to win by six lengths. In total he won six races and ran second in the Derby. In the Guineas, oddly he refused to corner and ran out to the other side of the track, which cost him valuable lengths, but despite this he managed to move from last position up to fourth at the finish.

A unique attribute that Highborn Harry had was his total disregard for distance – five furlongs or a mile and a half were all the same to him. Despite his growing success I felt my training skills were not up to knowing how to cope with this headstrong colt and so I asked my friend Terrance Millard to take him over. I just felt it was only fair to Highborn Harry that I find a trainer who had the expertise to handle such a difficult colt and tap into his full potential. Tragically – maybe it was the heavy sand tracks on which he then ran and was not used to – he soon pulled a tendon and I then retired him to stud. Like a lunatic, I did not give him any top mares with which to breed, and instead I gave him the cast-offs; even so he managed to produce some good winners, until he got so badly kicked in the testicles that we had to have him neutered.

Naughty Nymph, the dam of Highborn Harry, only ran eight times. She was never unplaced in her first three races, then went on to win five races in a row. The laugh was on me because like most racing people I was superstitious and when she started her winning sequence I was wearing a winter suit and polo-necked jersey. Now that we had arrived into the heat of an African summer I was not willing to risk discarding her lucky suit for summer clothing, so I used to suffer unbearably. In fact one of her admirers came to me one day and said, 'I see every time she runs you wear the same winter clothing. Are you not dying of heat-stroke?'

I laughed light-heartedly and passed it off, not willing to admit to my superstitious nature. Soon after this I retired her to start the August stud season, and with a sigh of relief shed my winter wear in time for the summer.

CHAPTER

8

One of the greatest fillies I ever trained, if not the greatest, was my magnificent Marysa. Her birth was nothing short of a miracle – she was a jaundiced foal and our incredible vet, Jim Antrobus, telephoned around the world asking how he could safely transfuse her blood. When he failed to find an answer he asked me if it would be all right to call on Chris Barnard once again. On this occasion, Chris sent a team out from Groote Schuur (the hospital he made world famous with the world's first successful human heart transplant) and they took some blood from Marysa's dam, Macquarie, back to the hospital. As I understand, they then drained the white cells and returned the red blood cells in powdered form. Jim mixed the plasma with a saline solution that he then transfused into the foal. Thus, thanks to the brilliance of a genius veterinarian and a genius heart surgeon, the world's first safe blood transfusion on a foal was performed on this farm.

Marysa grew into a perfectly beautiful filly. She was a rich bay with a wonderful head, shoulders and quarters, slightly back at the knee, but that was a defect that never worried me. With my wonderful training tracks and the Percy Sykes maxim never to gallop them until the epiphyses in the knees had closed, these setbacks were negligible. She went on to win 11 races and had 15 places, all in stakes races, and she was a champion five and six furlong specialist. Most of the time she ran against the colts, as she liked to come from behind and the fillies were not strong enough to set the fast pace she required.

Marysa became a racing icon and I became known to the enthusiastic racing public as 'Mama Marysa'. They waved to me from buses, from African taxis – and on the telephone, if I ever had to give my name away, there was often a stunned silence, then a startled voice would ask '… am I talking to Mama Marysa?' What then ensued was a long conversation on how much money the person had made and a request for a little insider information as to where she was next set to race. Marysa was getting on by this stage and was already four. I never raced my fillies beyond their fifth birthdays so there was just enough time to send Marysa off for a triumphant end to her racing career.

Before taking her to Durban for the Natalia Stakes, I had to give her a race in Cape Town, and as her blood reading showed that she was not 100 per cent fit, I needed a hard race to bring her along, as this always helped to improve the blood readings. It was the feature race, the Stewards Cup, and the top trainer, Theo de Klerk, had a very good colt entered. As usual, Marysa was a hot favourite in the forecast betting, but given her blood readings I worried for her fans, so I informed the public via the press that it wasn't that I thought she could not win, but she needed this race to get her fit and ready for the Natalia Stakes in Durban.

My announcement caused her to drift quickly out in the betting and when race day came Frank, who loved a good risk, commented that she looked magnificent and he was going to back her. He apparently had a huge bet and Marysa, who hated being beaten, just managed to get her nose in front on the winning post and won in a photo-finish.

Chaos reigned and I was escorted to the winning enclosure where the crowd was in a fury. They thought I had misinformed the press on purpose and quickly forgot all the times I had tipped my unbeatable horses to the press, even the first-timers. The stipendiary stewards said I was never to announce winners, predictions or otherwise to the press ever again.

When I went to the stewards' quarters to accept the trophy the area was practically deserted. I could see that it was with the greatest reluctance that someone had to hand over the huge silver cup and make a bit of a speech to someone they now thought had arranged a gambling coup on the famous Marysa at the expense of the racing public. As uncomfortable as this all was, it was soon forgotten as Marysa charged ahead of everyone and won her last race, the Durban Natalia Stakes – and I kept my winning opinions to myself from that point on.

Like all my other great fillies, Marysa returned to the Cape on a winning note and retired to stud. I then had time to reflect upon her racing history and the fact that without the knowledge of racing haematology, she probably would not have won all those great races. She carried a very low potassium level – and unless your potassium levels are correct, you tire badly and cannot find that extra energy to get you flying past your opposition. It is one of the most important readings in your racing blood: if any of my horses had depleted potassium levels I would give them a potassium drip.

Marysa never produced top horses like the others. I kept her daughter, Lady Marysa, who won three races and produced a black type winner, but like her dam, she also carried low potassium levels. I used to warn the trainers who bought the progeny of this defect, but none of them seemed to have heard of potassium levels and were not at all interested.

* * *

In those early days of Broadlands, Terrance Millard was the only other trainer looking at blood readings. He was however only doing three tests – HB (haemoglobin), PCV (packed cell volume) and ESR (erythrocyte sedimentation rate) – all of which were way ahead of the time. Terrance and his wife Joyce became great friends of mine; their son Tony, who I watched grow up, has now become a famous trainer in his own right and is based in Hong Kong. They also had two lovely daughters, one of whom married Geoff Woodruff, who went on to become another famous South African trainer. Jennifer, the eldest daughter, very sadly had a fatal accident on 13 November 1983.

The Millards had a lovely house and training facilities overlooking the beach at Blouberg. It was from here that Jennifer and her boyfriend Richard Hugh Best set sail on their Hobie Cat catamaran early one morning, as they often did. But that morning the weather changed quickly and the waves became mountainous. Richard gave

Jennifer his life jacket, although she already had one, and tied her to the mast. Then in an obvious heroic effort to save them both, he tried to steer for shore.

Sea Rescue searched from the water and air, but could not find them. Her parents were desperate. Tragically, Jennifer's body was washed ashore three days later, while Richard's was never found. No parent can ever fully recover from such a loss and my heart went out to Joyce and Terrance daily. Then many years later, my beloved friend lost his adored wife to Alzheimer's. He kept her at home with carers, so that he could be with her and help look after her. Sadly, as the disease progressed he had to take her to hospital, but would spend a great deal of time with her every day. One morning, Terrance called me and said, 'Pat, I have got to talk to you – Joyce has just died. When I was with her yesterday, she did not even recognise me and the hospital called me this morning to say that I must come immediately. I went straight away but by the time I got there, she had already died. I do not know how I am going to live without her. I have loved her all my life, I was 18 when I asked her to marry me and she has been the love of my life ever since. I cannot live in this house any longer, it has too many memories.' I was so deeply moved by his words of love and loss and at the same time rejoiced for them both and the love that they sustained for so many years.

* * *

Another world first took place here at Broadlands in 1980. One of my Australian mares, Dinah Dee, gave birth to a foal suffering from immune erythrolysis, which means that the blood from the

TOP: The day of my second wedding to Frank, Nairobi, 17 November 1970, together with Enid and Caryll.

ABOVE: In the registry office – Pat, Frank and Enid signing the register.

LEFT: Posing with one of the Broadlands peacocks beside the swimming pool, scene of many leisurely and enjoyable lunches.

TOP: Lunchtime by the pool with Bobby – baby baboons always loved the salad decoration at the side of the sandwich.

BOTTOM: Baloo arrived as a baby in 1982. Together with Buster, she saved my life, and I am forever indebted to her.

A loving hug is what all creatures need. CLOCKWISE FROM TOP LEFT: Pat with Bingo, with Larry *(Carolyn Koopmans/ Cape Argus)*, and with Kalu.

TOP LEFT: With one of the scarlet macaws rescued from the Indian market in Durban, and a baby baboon called Calvinia.

TOP RIGHT: One of my dogs, River – so called because she was rescued from one – in the Broadlands sitting room.

ABOVE: Soaking up some sunlight on the Broadlands stoep. *From left:* Pick n Pay, Honey and Bongo outside Pat's office, previously the dining room.

TOP: Morgan, Pat, Shelagh and dogs too numerous to mention on the front steps of Broadlands.

BOTTOM: A very special wedding. *From left:* Craig Carey, Amanda Shorter, Wakamba, Pat and Watusi. The Great Danes were named after two Kenyan tribes.

More than anything, a baby baboon needs close contact and security:

Evelyn, who has since sadly passed away, took it in her stride as cook.

Frank cheerfully does his bit.

A pastel portrait of Kalu.

All the Broadlands children, Simpiwe included, loved playing with the baboons.

Baloo on the river bank where she saved my life.

RIGHT: Just back from a walk! Amanda's retinue fills the Broadlands hallway.

BOTTOM: One of my rescued caracals – kittens are often found after their mothers have been poisoned or shot by farmers.

TOP: At home with my wonderful husband Frank, who spends three months of the year at Broadlands and the rest of the year in Australia.

BOTTOM: In the living room with my art collection and Nguni the Great Dane.

Views of Broadlands: Drivers passing on the N2 below Broadlands used to get a lovely view of the manor house as it sat on a rise, with the magnificent Hottentots Holland Mountains as a backdrop, and the paddocks, with all their white fencing and flowers, as a frame.

RIGHT: My baboons only had to take one look at Morgan and I was instantly forgotten! I always tease him, saying, 'I hope you don't get too conceited, as they are only looking for fleas: you are obviously covered in them.'

ABOVE: Kalu with Jimmy, her first keeper.

RIGHT: Jim Antrobus, our wonderful vet, always took time to play with Kalu when he came to look at the horses.

Bingo as a baby.

TOP: With Pat.

MIDDLE: With Pick n Pay.

BOTTOM: With Justin, Amanda's son and Pat's godson. They grew up sharing bottles, and as Justin grew older he was taken for rides on Kalu's back – all, for him, the order of the day!

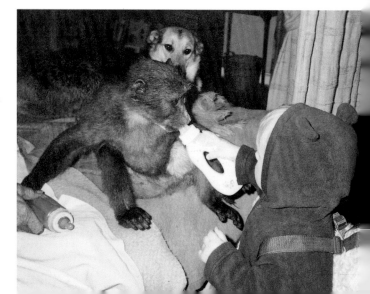

LEFT: My car full of dogs and baboons became a well-known sight in the supermarket car park and whoever was the latest baby – Bingo here – would have to accompany me while I was doing the shopping.

BELOW: Comfortable on the sofa – Pat, Morgan, dogs and sheep.

LEFT: Head-to head, Pat and Baloo.

MIDDLE LEFT: Kalu shares her enclosure with several beloved goats.

MIDDLE RIGHT: Kalu with her adored Amanda.

BOTTOM: The macaws I rescued from the Indian market became a great feature at Broadlands, as once they were acclimatised I let them loose to fly about as they pleased.

OPPOSITE PAGE:

TOP: Pat and Lady in the background; Elgin face-to-face with the camera. *(Carmen Nelstein)*

BOTTOM LEFT: Hans Britz stops to greet a baby baboon.

BOTTOM RIGHT: Elgin draped comfortably over a garden urn. *(Carmen Nelstein)*

Scenes from Kalu's life. She is madly in love with Michael Taperesu, her keeper, and gets quite frantic if he goes away for a night. *(Sam Reinders)*

foal, for some reason (usually through the placenta), gets into the mare's bloodstream. The mare then produces antibodies to fight the foal's blood and when the foal suckles the mare, the antibodies are absorbed and start to attack and destroy the foal's own red blood cells. Despite 28 blood transfusions from various mares as well as a complete exchange transfusion, where blood is removed and new blood added – this procedure was done very slowly, with 500 ml of blood going out and 500 ml of blood going in simultaneously – the foal eventually died of kidney failure.

Jim, our beloved vet, had called around the world and nobody had come up with a solution, so once again he asked if he could call my friend Chris Barnard to ask him for a prognosis. Chris suggested that next time he should take the mare's blood and wash it with saline solution before returning it to the infected foal. Using this procedure, many foals were then saved.

The following year, in 1981, Marysa was in foal for the first time and we were all terribly excited. However this was marred somewhat by concern over the number of cases of biliary that kept occurring on the farm. Jim, in consultation with Hans, discovered that when he was bleeding the pregnant mares for progesterone level determination, he was using the same needle on four to five mares at a time. Jim then concluded that it had to be one of the mares who was the carrier – and, to his utter horror, he discovered it was Marysa, whose foal (Lady Marysa) was then born with biliary fever.

The foal, unsurprisingly, was very ill, but this time Jim was prepared and called Chris Barnard right away. Chris then sent a team out from Groote Schuur Hospital and they made a decision to remove serum and give Lady Marysa a dose of concentrated red blood cells. I remember seeing the blood arriving back looking like a thick yellow powder and how Jim mixed it with the saline solution before transfusing it. Once the transfusion was complete Lady Marysa made an astounding recovery.

A few years later Marysa had another foaling problem, this time it was dystocia, with the foal malpositioned in the uterus. Time is of the essence in cases like this as a vet needs to give the mare an injection to stop the contractions before the foal suffers oxygen deprivation and dies. We were about 60 km away from Jim's hospital and tragically the foal died on arrival. Jim removed the foal under general anaesthetic; however Marysa's placenta was retained and within 72 hours she had developed acute laminitis. Jim had heard of a similar case in the United States, where they had reported the successful use of dimethyl sulfoxide (DMSO), so based on this he decided to give her three transfusions daily – it was a foul-smelling concoction that permeated the whole stable yard, but the result was that Marysa, with the help of our wonderful Hans, recovered extremely well.

Another remarkable thing happened in 1984 when Royal Glitter, another of my very good race mares, was found one morning lying in the paddock in great pain. Jim deduced that she had been bitten by either a snake or a poisonous spider, as on examination he found a necrotic area on the pastern which had developed into a large ulcerative wound with a crater and dead tissue. She underwent three surgeries and her flexor tendons became infected. It was decided that humane euthanasia was to be the inevitable conclusion. Then, as luck would have it, my dear friend Graham Viney came to lunch one day and told me how his orthopaedic surgeon, Dr John May, had cured him of much the same thing. Jim contacted Dr May, who told him that when humans have an infection in their dead tissue, slow-release gentamycin beads were inserted into the area and this promoted the chances of a full recovery. The beads came in a string – rather like a string of pearls, I thought as I watched Jim insert them into Royal Glitter's infected tendon area. Once again, another of my horses made a full recovery!

Another South African first for Broadlands was when the first human ultrasound machine used for pregnant women was tried out on Miss International. Jim Antrobus's hospital team arrived and, in my medical room, scanned Miss International's uterus, and there was then great excitement at what they could see. Shortly after this Jim went on holiday to Australia, where he had heard they had an ultrasound machine designed especially for horses. He arrived home with one in hand and the result was nothing short of amazing. One could actually see the follicles, and when I first saw the tiny little outline which Jim explained was the foal, the excitement was always incredible.

CHAPTER

9

When I first attended the yearling sales here in South Africa, I was amazed at how badly turned out most of the yearlings were. I had been used to the immaculate stables of my stepfather, Lord Furness, where every horse had four of everything, to ensure there were no marks, all in the Furness colours of plum and gold. Even his huge grey Percherons, with their shining silver manes and tails and their hooves beautifully polished, looked as if they were about to leave for the show ring as they set off to work in the fields. I would watch in horror as some of the top studs had not even bothered to groom their yearlings, who were brought straight out of the camps with knotted manes and tails, some with baling wire for bits on their halters. Not only that, but the grooms leading them were dressed like tramps. It was an absolute eye-opener.

When I took my first lot of yearlings to the sale, they certainly stood out from the crowd as they had all been beautifully groomed and were the only ones with bright shiny coats and beautiful quarter marks. Their feet were polished and their halters, made with pale blue and white headbands to match the Broadlands colours, were eye-catching, to say the least. The grooms wore pale blue track suits with Broadlands printed in big letters on the back and on their heads they had knitted blue and white caps with pompoms. I don't think the crowd in the stands could quite believe it, or perhaps even understand it at that time.

According to Percy Sykes's theory, which I had followed religiously, one had to keep increasing the feed by a scoop a month leading up to the sales and lunge the yearlings every day to build up their muscle. So of course all my yearlings were bigger, very muscled up, and with their shining coats looked like a lot of film stars. The breeders and trainers looked askance at this influx of beautifully bred yearlings. It had already become common knowledge that all the horses were stabled at night and fed proper feed! Not many had praise for these training tactics: the word on the track was that this crazy woman was upsetting all the breeding and racing norms, and the result would be a lot of soft horses that would never stand up to racing.

Over the years, though, things changed: with my incredible race fillies and their progeny doing so well, everyone had to concede that there was some sense to my so-called crazy approach, especially when on several occasions we topped the select sale.

* * *

While I was training, a lovely English couple who became very interested in racing used to get up early in the mornings to come and watch the gallops each week, before going on to have breakfast. I got to know them as they were always at the races and used to bet on my horses whenever I told them to. One day the man, whose name was William, said to me, 'Pat, I am not very rich and I really don't have much money, but if you can find me a cheap yearling colt that you like, please buy him for me.'

In my yearly wanderings around the studs, I think it was on Frank Freeman's farm that I came across a lovely little chestnut colt. I managed to buy him straight off the farm as a yearling for R10 000. On behalf of his new owners, I named him Sir William.

Now, with the excitement of a horse of their own, they never missed a gallop and after breakfast they would spend the rest of the morning with their beloved Sir William, sitting with him in the paddock and feeding him carrots.

Sir William was a beautiful chestnut colt, not very big, but all muscle, and he had a lovely affectionate nature. He was always hanging his head over the door of his stable in search of treats – which of course his loving owners used to shower him with, in between hugs and kisses.

Once he became a two-year-old and started training, they would come out to the farm twice a week for his workouts, and when he went to Kenilworth racecourse for his final preparation gallops, they insisted on always accompanying him in the horse box. The great day of his first race as a two-year-old arrived and I had placed him in a field where it was almost impossible – with the way he was working and with his spot-on blood count – for him to get beaten.

I told them that I could almost guarantee he would win. The excitement was intense: afterwards William's wife told me that he had not slept for two nights and had to take a tranquilliser and a sleeping pill. We had a very early lunch up at the steward's quarters, as Frank had now become a steward of the Jockey Club, and then I escorted them down to the paddock and went to see Sir William being saddled.

He came into the paddock looking like a little film star, full of bounce and so pleased with himself. His groom was smartly dressed in his Broadlands colours and Sir William, with his smart bridle and pale blue and white headband, looked pretty as a picture.

Then, like the true little champion he was, he charged ahead to the finishing line and won his very first race. We watched from the steward's quarters and the screams of joy from his proud owners as they watched Sir William charge to the front almost deafened me. There was then a wild surge to get to the lift, in order to meet Sir William and lead him into the winning enclosure. Tears of joy flowed as they rushed down to meet their little hero – they were so anxious to be there in time for the lead-in; then, one on either side of Sir William, they proudly led him into the winning enclosure.

Afterwards in the steward's quarters, while celebrating with champagne, William announced that this day along with his wedding day were the two greatest days of his life. A messenger then came to inform us that the horse was now ready to go home. They rushed down so as to be with him and once again Sir William was smothered in hugs and kisses and tears of joy as they accompanied him out to the horsebox. They then insisted on being 'up close and personal' with their pride and joy and so joined the horse box as he was driven back to the farm. On a congratulatory note, we always used to send the racehorses home with a net full of lucerne, but Sir William I gather had hardly any time to eat his fodder, between the hugs, the carrots and sugar cubes that kept coming his way. It didn't stop there, with the still elated William and his wife wanting to camp out in Sir William's stable for the night, but I quickly discouraged this as I could not see Sir William getting much sleep, which is essential for a racehorse and even more so after a race well won.

Sir William went on to win an additional five races. I had to stop racing him for a while, as his owner William himself had had a heart attack and was in hospital for quite some time. Once William had recovered, he and his wife used to come out to Broadlands almost every day to have breakfast and lunch with us and talk about nothing else except their beloved Sir William.

By this time Sir William was back in training and a few months later was ready to race. Race day arrived and as usual they accompanied him in the horse box. Sir William was in fine form, his blood readings were perfect and I expected him to win. Not wanting to be so far from Sir William again, his owners decided that to be up in the steward's quarters while he raced was just too far away from their beloved. So they chose to forego lunch and instead have a snack at the café by the paddock – just so they could see him and be with him while he was being saddled. Then we always watched him run sitting on a large wooden stand opposite the winning post.

On this occasion, Sir William, as I predicted, once again surged to the front and won by a length and a half. William, his owner, who was standing beside me screaming with delight, suddenly gave a great groan and collapsed. He died on the grandstand and there was nothing the doctors could do. But I always thought, if you have to die, which we all do, what a wonderful way to go – all in a moment filled with such joy.

CHAPTER

10

In the days of my beloved mother, she always used to take Tikki, her adored tree hyrax, with her everywhere. She had had him for 20 years, and he went all over the world with her. There were other hyraxes after Tikki, but as they were called Tikki too it was as if they were the same one. In the days of Furness and his private planes, trains and ocean-going liners, it was no problem, but after his death, when we travelled by ship and airliners, it was more difficult. Tikki even accompanied Mummy to the nursing home in London when she had to have an operation. I was the one always being sent out to get his bamboo shoots, rose petals and various other delicacies; he was the bane of my existence. He spent most of his days round her neck; she used to have special jackets made by her friend Coco Chanel to keep the hyrax hidden when necessary. As a child, horribly embarrassed by the attention attracted, I had promised myself time and again that never, but never, would I have wild animals or parrots. How little did I know! If anything, I suppose I have proved to be a great deal worse than Mummy.

Since arriving in South Africa, she had acquired another companion, a rescued meerkat. This creature had a tiny collar and lead and when she went racing, the meerkat would always accompany her. As Mummy could not take both animals up to the steward's quarters for lunch, the meerkat used to be left in the ladies' room, with the lady attendant in charge. Years after my mother's death, the lady attendant got talking to me one day and said how much she had adored my mother and how she missed her. She told me that leaving 'Kit I Kat' with her was such an honour and that the ladies who came into the ladies' room used to be amazed at first, then when they got to know him, he became the centre of attention and they used to bring him titbits in their handbags. He adored all the kissing and cuddling and female attention. In addition to this, she told me that at the end of the day she used to get a fortune in tips from my mother. Those days were the highlights of her life and she told me just how much she missed them – it was always heartwarming to hear how my mother lived on in people's memories.

On the odd occasion I would take one of my rescued animals to the races. One time I took a little blind baboon called Brixley. The whole troop to which she had once belonged had been poisoned by some awful farmer, resulting in Brixley's mother dying and Brixley being blinded. She was so small she needed regular nappy changes and bottle feeds every few hours, which is why she had to come with me.

On this occasion, I had taken Brixley out of my carrier bag and put her on my lap while I was having some sandwiches for lunch in the tea room, which in those days was right by the saddling enclosure and paddock. Some crisp lettuce and freshly grated carrots accompanied the sandwiches for some decoration and this fact was not missed by Brixley, whose tiny little hand kept reaching up and groping for little fistfuls of carrot. I was delighted as this meant she was getting a diet beyond her normal Lactogen baby formula, so I asked for extra grated carrot, much to Brixley's delight! Our very nice waiter, who always looked after us on race day, was utterly thrilled with the new lunch guest

Soon other people in the tea room started noticing the tiny hairy hand stretching out of my lap in search of more grated carrot. The women especially were fascinated and I saw them asking our waiter and being assured it was a blind baby baboon, not a deformed child. A few of them then approached me wanting to see this tiny thing and naturally they all wanted to hold her, which of course was not possible as baby baboons cling to their mother and scream with fright if separated from their security for even a few seconds. In Brixley's case this was even more apparent as she had already lost one mother and was not going to risk losing another.

Almost the whole tea room was enchanted by the little visitor apart from one horrible man, probably a farmer, who insisted that all baboons were vermin. We had quite an argument and I told him that if anyone is vermin it is the human race that destroys forests, poisons and shoots animals as well as each other, and all in the name of fun. The undying love and loyalty of animals is something you do not often see in mankind. Therefore, on the whole I prefer the company of my many animals to that of a crowd of people.

On another occasion I took my baby crow, Jackie, who I had to

handfeed out of my carrier bag. Having procured some hot water to mix with his ProNutro, I was opening his beak to feed him
when someone came over to talk to me and in a moment of inat-
tention, he hopped out of the bag and onto the floor. Soon the
whole tearoom erupted into chaos as everyone came to my rescue
trying to catch Jackie, who was happily hopping from the underneath of one table to another. It was quite hard to spot the black
crow in the dark under the tables, but eventually a very nice young
man climbed under his table and rescued my errant bird for me.
Following the crow fiasco, a woman approached me and said how
much she enjoyed it when I was in the tea room; one never knew
what would happen next.

* * *

Horse racing was the most popular sport of the day in South Africa
and with this came much excitement and glamour. On Met days,
everyone used to spend a fortune on hats, beautiful dresses and
glamorous suits. Every year I would hire a huge pavilion tent for all
our lunch guests; these tents became one of the features of Met day
and they used to line the rails. Kenilworth Racecourse employed
a garden expert and the paddock and the entire surrounds had
magnificent flowers and hedges all adding to the colourful event!
Of course, the lunch parties with their unlimited booze and food
would sometimes go on to nightfall.

Getting these Met day parties together was quite an undertak-
ing. I used to hire caterers but I still had to decide on the menu and
make sure the decorations were all in place. Then buying enough
alcohol to cater for over 100 guests as well as the casual visitors

was quite a headache. One had to get there really early and was unable to leave until the last guest had departed.

I remember one particular occasion when one of the guests and a friend had gone to relieve themselves in one of the nearby flower beds, as our own toilet facilities were full at the time and they were in a hurry to return to the festivities. Unbeknown to them, one of the other guests had passed out in the very flower bed they chose to visit and he only came to when he got covered in a shower of urine. The unfortunate and intoxicated man had to be taken to the men's room and washed down; he was then lent a jacket by one of our kind waiters and driven safely home.

The drunken revelry I witnessed at these events never ceased to amaze me. I have never been keen on alcohol myself, with two glasses of champagne being my limit. I am sure this is a result of a terrible mistake I made when I was about 10 and living at Sandley House. I had come back from riding and, feeling hot and thirsty, seen in the butler's pantry a lovely jug of what looked like delicious fruit juice. I drank the lot – needless to say it was Pimms! I got horribly drunk and sick and I also received a thrashing from my governess. After that experience I was put off alcohol for life. My mother also hated alcohol, so that might have been an additional influence.

In addition to the big Met parties we hosted, Broadlands was also a renowned venue when it came to entertaining. Famous faces who were cherished friends were the norm at the lunch table. Earl Spencer, Lady Diana's good-looking younger brother, would often join us here with his family and like his sister he was so marvellous with children, constantly playing with them and cuddling and kissing them – they were so loved and it was such a pleasure to spend time with them all.

A very funny incident occurred here at Broadlands when HRH

the Duke of Gloucester was invited to lunch along with some other royal faces. The duke's mother had been a great friend of my mother's and she had stayed with Mummy in Kenya on several occasions before she married the Duke of Gloucester. I still have two lovely small Kenya landscapes that she painted during this period. His father, prior to marrying his mother, had been very much in love with Beryl Markham and the old Queen Mother, Queen Mary (the present Queen's grandmother) had paid Beryl a large stipend at the time to stop her marrying her son. I did not know if the duke knew about his father's early love life – and if he did, would he have come to lunch if he knew of my close relationship with Beryl? To complicate matters, as I was arranging the placements for lunch, my friend Graham Viney cautioned me not to place Lord Spencer and the duke near each other, as they were not the best of friends! I now had to rearrange all the table settings and to balance things out, I placed one at one head of the table and the other at the other head of the table. Thankfully it was a very long yellowwood table that Mummy had ordered when we first arrived at Broadlands, so long that a donkey cart had to be used to bring it up to the house.

At the time I seemed to remember that one is not supposed to walk in front of a member of the royal family, so I was busy trying to get the duke from the sitting room to the dining room, which was quite a distance, without leading the way. In my efforts to do so and feeling rather clumsy in my panic to do the right thing, I tripped over one of the dogs. To my great relief, one of the guests following close behind grabbed me and stopped me falling into the royal arms.

Thankfully lunch went off smoothly and the duke was easy to talk to. He was quick to bring up the subject of Beryl, as he understood I knew her quite well. So I gave him all the juicy details, telling him his father was in the end a fortunate man to have his mother Queen Mary pay Beryl to stay away. Thankfully Beryl's love of money ensured she did, as the marriage would have been a disaster.

The next royals to come to lunch were Prince and Princess Michael of Kent. This was in 1993 and they were absolutely charming guests. The princess had written a wonderful book called *Cupid and the King*, about five of Europe's most celebrated royal mistresses. She later inscribed and sent a copy to me, mentioning the wonderful day they had spent at Broadlands. Another guest linked to royalty who came to lunch a number of times was Andrew Parker Bowles, the former husband of Prince Charles's great love, Camilla Parker Bowles. He too was absolutely charming and I do believe he and his wife Rosemary attended the wedding of Prince Charles and Camilla.

CHAPTER

11

When I decided it was time to bring some stallions to Broadlands, my first import was Adamastor, a French 2000 Guineas winner. I think he may have been the first overseas classic winner to come to this country. He was beautiful and had such a gentle nature. I used to take him for walks with the dogs and baboons, but he never turned out to be a great sire. One unforgettable experience with Adamastor was the time that we had a lot of very famous international jockeys for lunch, amongst whom was Yves Saint Martin. Hearing that Adamastor was on the farm, he was so excited and said that he had been his first classic winner.

After lunch we all went down to the stable yard, where Yves saw Adamastor grazing in his camp. He strode over to him and then to my utter amazement, without so much as a saddle, bridle or even a halter, he leaped up onto his back, put his arms around his neck and gave him a kiss and a hug. Given the tendency for any race horse to be startled and to rear up, I thought it was an incredibly brave thing to do.

I decided that Broadlands was definitely in need of a top-class stallion. There was a stallion sale in England coming up and I had picked out a horse called Royal Prerogative from the catalogue. One of the main reasons I had selected him was that he had my mother's Oaks winner in his female line. He was also a great miler, having won the Royal Hunt Cup amongst a number of other wins. As I was not there at the time, I asked a friend who was a well-known English veterinary surgeon to go and take a look at Royal Prerogative. He called me back right away and said, 'This is a horse that is magnificent to look at and has faultless conformation. I cannot recommend him more highly.' So I decided to take the plunge. Although he cost a fortune, I was determined to get him.

I was indeed fortunate in this regard, as only one vote kept him from going to the National Stud, and then I had to outbid a Japanese buyer. For a million pounds sterling, he was finally mine.

When the great Royal Prerogative arrived in South Africa, our neighbour, Gurd van Heesch, who had tossed Frank for Rose Bay, asked if he could have a half share in the stallion. I readily agreed to this, as it helped with the financial side of things. Royal Prerogative was indeed magnificent, a rich chestnut with a glorious head and conformation and he had a character to match as he was wonderfully affectionate and unfazed by my many animals. He was to become an incredible stallion – a 14 times champion brood mare sire, which was unheard of at the time.

I often went over to the stable yard at night and lay beside him in the deep straw of his stable. He would nicker at me as I entered and I would cuddle up to him for an hour or so with my arm around his neck, stroking him and every so often feeding him sugar lumps.

His stable opened up onto a paddock, which he could go in or out of as he chose. All my stallions had the same facilities, as I was horrified when I first came to South Africa and saw how, on most of the big stud farms, the stallions were kept in all day and just taken out for walks. Not my beloveds – they had to have their freedom of choice.

Hans Britz, who at this stage had become too heavy to ride and left the racing stable, became Royal Prerogative's personal attendant at the stud and looked after him as if he was a child. He also adored him and we often used to joke about Royal Prerogative's covering idiosyncrasies. It would take him ages before he would so much as look at the mare. Then, when he finally did, he would turn around and try to lead Hans back into his box. On other occasions he would decide to cover the presented mare without too much persuasion – he was clearly attracted to some mares and not others.

While he was a very fertile horse, I never let him cover more than two mares a day. I followed Percy Sykes's maxim that it takes eight hours before the semen fully recovers its potency. On the very odd occasion when the demand was high and the mares were all ready at the same time I would get Royal Prerogative to cover three mares in a day. Hans would then lecture me endlessly, saying, 'Miss Pat, you can't do this to my boy, it's not good for him, it is just being greedy!' I would then try and convince him that it just had to be done, as Jim had checked the follicles in all three waiting mares and they were ready to ovulate. Hans was never happy about this, such was his love for the stallion. As far as he was concerned, there was only one superior being on the farm – and this was not myself; it was Royal Prerogative.

When Royal Prerogative first arrived, the great stud owner Paule de Wet, who owned Zandvliet Stud in Ashton, came to the farm to see this priceless stallion. At that time he was by far the most expensive stallion ever to come to South Africa. Paule was always a laugh a minute and as he was leaving, he took off his hat and sweeping it to his chest as he bowed low in front of me, he said, 'My dear young lady, this is a beautiful horse, but no sire in this country warrants that price. I think you have rather overdone it this time!' Thank heavens he was wrong and I had not – with his very first crop Royal Prerogative produced classic winners and from then on never stopped.

* * *

A phone call came through one day from Frank, who was in Australia. He had recently lost all his money through bad investments so I was initially speechless when he told me that he had just come from the Sydney sales and had bought a beautiful stallion called Averof for $700 000. I told him he was mad; we had enough stallions and I was certainly not forking out $700 000 on a stallion I did not know anything about. 'Too bad,' was Frank's response, 'I've already bought him; therefore you must send the money out.'

Well, what an absolute champion Averof turned out to be! Not only was he magnificent to look at, but he was 16.2 hands full of muscular perfection. He was to become another champion sire; Averof and Royal Prerogative together were an incredible combination.

Through Royal Prerogative, I met John Freeman. He and his father were bloodstock agents and they too came to see the supposedly overpriced stallion that they had heard so much about. I took them down to see our beautiful boy, who was in his stable eating out of his manger. Waiting for Hans to bring his halter and lead, I lifted his head up and gave him a couple of kisses and some sugar cubes. John commented that he had never seen a stallion being treated like a pet before! The Freemans lived in Johannesburg and I became great friends with John, having lunch or dinner with them whenever I went that way for the sales. On one occasion they invited me to join them on a friend's boat on Kariba Dam in Zimbabwe. Everything was going very well but I had on an impractical pair of shoes and found myself sliding down the bank as I headed towards the boat. The result was a badly cut chin, two bottom teeth and one top tooth knocked out. I was then stitched up at the local hospital – the memory of how filthy the place was is still fresh in my mind!

After years of having this marvellous stallion reigning supreme, tragedy struck. The feed companies had bought in some contaminated food and yearlings and horses were starting to die on the various studs. My beloved Royal Prerogative was one of them. By the time the vets had discovered the reason for the deaths, the contaminated food had started affecting the horses' livers. Jim, being the incredible vet he is, did everything he could to save Royal Prerogative. He even asked Brian Baker to come down from Durban as well as another well-known vet, Frikkie du Preez, whose opinion he very much respected, to see if they could come up with anything.

Like a coward, I kept away; I just could not bear to see Royal Prerogative struggling for his life. I kept telling myself that while there is life there is hope. When I realised that of life there was very little hope for my adored stallion, I practically crawled back on my hands and knees to apologise to him. I spent most nights lying beside him, talking to him and telling him of my love. I just could not give Jim the fatal words that would have ended his life. He did not seem to be actually suffering, just getting weaker and weaker. I used to creep out before dawn broke and return to my room, so that nobody would know. I had enough of a reputation in the racing world of being a lunatic.

When the terrible day came, we were all with him and our tears flowed as Jim put him to sleep. Royal Prerogative was buried outside his camp and I had a big tombstone dedicated to him, which I had put on top of his grave. This way his memory and how he broke an all South African record when he became South African champion brood mare sire 14 times would live on for ever at Broadlands.

* * *

Jim Antrobus became world famous with some of the work he did on this farm and unsurprisingly Antony Beck soon came to me and asked if Jim could work for them too. The Becks are a famous South African family; not only in the horse world, but Antony's father Graham at one time owned an enormous coal empire. He also owned Stuttafords, which is the South African equivalent of the English Harrods, albeit on a slightly smaller scale. Apart from their famous stud farms, the Becks have a famous wine farm, which interestingly enough provided the sparkling wine for President Obama's inauguration.

Through my friendship with Graham and Rhona Beck, whom I met soon after I arrived in South Africa, I got to know their younger son, Antony, very well. I was one of the guests at his eighteenth birthday party and he used to come and visit at least two or three times a week. We used to talk about racing and breeding all the time; he was always very interested in what I was doing and the success I was having with my racehorses. He also loved all my weird and wonderful animals. I in turn looked upon him as the son I never had. I was always so impressed that such a rich young man should be so unspoilt and kind.

I will always remember when on one occasion I had run out of lucerne for my horses because of a late delivery. I called up Antony and asked if they could let me have some in the meantime. Later that day I saw an enormous truck load of lucerne trundling up the long driveway – and driven by Antony Beck! All their drivers had been busy and as he was determined not to let me down, he made the three-hour journey over a mountain pass himself.

Today, all these years later, he is still such a marvellous person. I do not see him so often nowadays as he lives on his famous stud farm, Gainesway, in Kentucky with his lovely American wife and their children. However when he is in South Africa he always comes to see me.

This was not the first or the last time that the Beck family came to my rescue; little did I know that one day Graham's generosity would save me when I nearly lost the farm and that a few years after that Antony and Rhona would also come to my rescue and enable me to keep Broadlands going.

Another wonderful chapter in my life was the day I first heard about Kalu. It was in 1990 and a friend of mine, Maluli Lomba, called me up. She told me that a friend of hers who was the Argentine Consulate General in Zaïre (now DRC) had, like most other foreign residents, had to leave the country due to the escalating conflict. In doing so they had to leave behind the precious baby chimpanzee they had rescued from the local market. Her name was Kalu and she had been left with the faithful staff, but how long they could manage to keep her no one knew. Would I be interested in taking her? I was delighted at the idea, never realising how long it would take and what an enormous amount of paperwork it would entail, with a trail involving government, airline and immigration officials as well as vets and animal protection agencies.

As a starting point, I had to get the South African government's permission to import a chimpanzee, and then I had to get blood tests done before she could leave Zaïre. These were for AIDS, TB and a host of other minimal risk diseases. Several months passed and I thought everything was on track but was then told I would have to get permission from CITES, the Convention on International Trade in Endangered Species of Wild Fauna and Flora. Finally, with a few contacts through friends and the recommendation that I had had a chimpanzee in Kenya, I was given the permit. Now flight arrangements had to be organised to bring her from Zaïre to Johannesburg. There she had to be met by the head of customs, as she had to be kept quarantined until she could come to the Western Cape; I had with the veterinary department's approval built a quarantine station on the farm.

We were all so excited when the great day arrived and Kalu was actually on the plane headed in this direction, but it came as quite a shock when I got the news that there was now an additional chimp on the plane, and one without a licence. It turned out that this 'extra' chimp was being smuggled by a Zaïrian government minister hoping to sell it for human experiments. Suddenly I found myself responsible for the pair of them and was told that I needed to get a permit from our local Nature Conservation authority to allow the other chimp to travel, as long as I guaranteed to find a home for it outside South Africa. Failing this they would both have to return to Zaïre to an unknown fate.

I started phoning around and very soon a family called the Siddels at Chimfunshi in Zambia agreed to take the chimp and so I quickly started organising her flight to Zambia. The plane landed in Johannesburg and the permit had still not arrived. The head of customs in Johannesburg was simply amazing and so practical. We were in constant telephonic contact: finally, when he said they could not hold the plane up any longer from its return to Zaïre, he reassured me that he would go with it to the take-off and I could call him immediately with the permit number if it should arrive. I was on my knees praying when the permit arrived and he was then able to unload the two chimps before the plane took off. The timing was quite simply miraculous, as was the help given by so many, from the marvellous head of customs, to my great friend the veterinary surgeon Mike Truscott who looked after them while in quarantine, to Nature Conservation for all the trouble they had gone to, and above all CITES, who rushed through the permit.

Finally Kalu arrived and was without a doubt destined to become another great love in my life. Had I known then how spoilt, demanding and bossy she was to become, I may well have sent her on her way that very day!

In terms of her quarantine regulations, Kalu had to remain in her quarantine station on the farm for a full three months. I had built a large indoor-outdoor caged area off my office. She had her bed raised, with a ladder up to it, as most chimpanzees do not like to sleep on the ground as they are arboreal animals. I also installed a television so that she could watch animal programmes. Not long after she got here I had to go to Kenya, so I left Amanda Shorter, a wonderful young girl who was now looking after my yearlings, in charge of this precious gift. Kalu was very insecure when she arrived, so Amanda used to sit in the cage with her every day.

After the three months' quarantine period I let Kalu loose so she could run around the farm. At night she would sleep in my bed with me and all the dogs and baboons, or back in her old bed, whichever she preferred. She spent her time with me, coming to the stables every day, though I suspect that this really provided an excuse to be near our wonderful vet Jim, who when he had finished his work with the mares, used to play with her and carry her around while she smothered him in hugs and kisses.

I used to walk around the farm every day, but unlike the baboons, Kalu would get bored after a while and insist on being given a piggyback ride home, so with her great hairy arms wrapped around my neck and legs around my waist, I used to have to hump this great weight about.

One of many funny incidents with Kalu occurred when we were coming through the yard one late afternoon. Shelagh noticed a very drunken worker trying to rake up the fallen leaves and Kalu, who had a great taste for alcohol, immediately realised that he smelt strongly of the stuff. I suppose, in the back of her mind, she thought he might be a possible source of supply for her. Kalu immediately rushed up behind him and prodded him in the back, whereupon he very drunkenly turned round to see a huge chimp right next to him. Letting out a scream of fear, he tried to fend her off with his rake, but this she snatched out of his hands and then head-butted him in the stomach. Being so drunk, he just fell over backwards and was now lying on the ground. Kalu then ambled over to him and put her nose right up against his mouth as she tried to smell his alcoholic breath, whereupon he let out another scream of fear and passed out.

Although Kalu often preferred the company of men, of course she absolutely adored Amanda. One day, Amanda had to rush up to our local Somerset West vet, Dr Denkhaus, to collect some medicine and as it was winter she dressed Kalu up in an anorak and jeans. As chimpanzees come from a tropical climate, Amanda always worried that she might catch a chill. She then put her on the front seat of her car, buckled her in and set off for Somerset West.

As they stopped at the traffic lights everybody started staring; they could not believe what they were seeing. Windows were opening and people were peering out; was it a monster child or a chimpanzee? They then passed a school with all the children coming out, which created another furore, as Kalu was so anxious to get out of the car and join them. She had wound down the window and was waving and talking to the children in chimp talk – much to their utter joy and amazement.

Amanda told me she was freaked out by the time she finally got Kalu to the vet, but in fact I think she enjoyed every minute, as she was always taking Kalu for drives. She often used to drive her down to the racing stables in the morning – and in those days if you came through the vineyard side, before we turned the area into horse paddocks, you had to cross the river, over which I had built a causeway. As you came out of the river crossing there was quite a steep bank on either side. For some reason, on this morning, Amanda had been concentrating on something else, and flew up the side of the bank. Kalu, when she saw what was happening, let out a cry of despair and hid on the floor with her hands over her eyes. After this, Amanda complained that Kalu never fully trusted her to drive with due care and attention. There seems to be some truth in this, as soon after, driving down Main Road in Somerset West with Kalu standing on the front seat watching the road behind, she suddenly saw a car approaching at great speed. Screeching frantically, she pointed to the back window, then because she thought Amanda was not paying enough attention, hit her over the head and threw herself onto the floor in a bundle of terror.

* * *

While Amanda was very close to Kalu, her primary role at Broadlands was with the horses.

Amanda had come out from England with her parents at the age of eight. She went to school here and both she and her sister Lisa were horse mad. They had their own horses and were both very good riders. They show jumped, had Western Province colours and they lived on a farm not far from us.

Janet Bayley had run my yearling barn very successfully for several years but on her mother's death she inherited a house and some money, so she decided to run a cat rescue operation. I was desperate for someone to run the yearling barn, but after a few attempts I had still not found what I was looking for. Most of the girls were more interested in sex than looking after yearlings – one young one used to have it off with the stable hands in the float on the way back from the sales, while another came screaming into the stud one morning saying that she had just slept with a man who ran a whorehouse and only told her the next morning that he also had AIDS. She was totally hysterical and then passed out. Not much was known about AIDS in those days, except that you died from it. Enough was enough; aside from being a sex maniac she was useless in the yearling barn.

Although Amanda was only 18 at the time, I offered her the job. It was 1987, and one of the best decisions I have ever made. As it turned out, she was brilliant and she fell in with all my ideas and added to them. She was also wonderful with all the dogs and cats and baboons. With Amanda in control, our yearlings became the shining lights of the sales.

Another of Amanda's tributes was that she was very good at lunging; to do this correctly is very important for building up a horse's muscle. The main thing is not to overdo the lunging, as a horse is working against itself as it travels around the ring. Five minutes maximum, with two and a half minutes a side, is the most a horse can manage.

Correct breaking in of a racehorse is very important. At home in England and Ireland, being young and a lightweight, when I was on one of Furness's studs, I used to be roped in to help break the horses in. First, they used to be lunged with just a girth on; then, once used to the girth, a few days later the saddle would be included. Following this, the halter would be added to which a bit had been attached, and not long after this the halter would be replaced by a bridle.

When they were used to this, the saddle would be girthed up a bit tighter. Finally a lightweight rider would be put up and the horse would be led by the groom around the lunge ring until it was happy with the new weight. Once this happened one would trot the horse in the lunge ring, being mindful to trot in both directions. When lunging this is vitally important as you don't want to build up muscle on one side more than the other.

Having been so strictly brought up with racehorses, I was horrified at some of the people who were so-called specialists in the business. I saw too many riders sawing the bit in the horse's mouth, and while the horse held its head high in protest, holding it in even tighter and then hitting from behind to get it to go faster – I couldn't bear to watch these riders as they butchered those young yearlings' mouths! Of course there were the other breakers-in who were very good. I also used to be horrified every time I went to the Milnerton early-morning gallops, seeing those poor two-year-olds moving through the heavy sand unsupervised with young men who had no real riding skills hanging onto their mouths and coming down heavily on their loins. How many bad backs and legs it must have given these youngsters I shudder to think!

* * *

Preparation for the yearling sales was a combined effort and involved a great deal of work.

Three months before the sale we continued to work them in the lunge ring and then we started to increase the feed by half a scoop a week. By the time they got to the sale they were on about 20 kg a day and they arrived looking strong and muscled up.

Plaiting the mane and the top of the tail was another thing we became known for. I could never plait, but Amanda was brilliant and in addition to this she would always make sure that the squares on their quarters were brushed and shining before they appeared in the ring.

One day on one of my shopping visits to my local supermarket, Checkers, I noticed a display of coloured rinses for women's hair and had the idea of using these rinses on the tails and manes of the yearlings. Silver rinses for the greys, I thought, would bring out an extra silvery shine. Glittery dresses were all the rage at the time and we had some superb yearlings to show off.

One of the yearlings was an incredibly beautiful grey colt called Kayani out of the champion race filly Breyani, by the champion sire Royal Prerogative; there was also a filly called Stolen Gem by Averof out of my beautiful Imperial Jade. This was a family with nothing but black type! I suggested to Amanda that as these two magnificent yearlings were appearing on the select night for the top pedigree yearlings, we should add a little sparkle to the sale. So off we headed to Checkers, where we loaded up with silver and black rinses and an array of glitter.

Kayani's dam, Breyani, had belonged to a great friend of mine, Ingrid Lubbe. As a young teenager Ingrid had been very ill and lying in hospital, had been reading the book *National Velvet*. Her eighteenth birthday was coming up and her father, on the family's daily visits, asked her what she would like as a present. Ingrid said she would like a filly that she could race. So her doting father went and got her a catalogue from the yearling sale, brought it back and told her to choose which one she would like. Ingrid decided on Breyani; she loved the name and the fact that the filly was a grey.

The magic of the story is that this lovely grey filly turned out to be a champion race filly. Ingrid, now well enough to go racing, but still not very strong, used to cry and practically collapse every time her darling filly won yet another race. It was on the racecourse that I met Ingrid; she was such a sweet girl and she often used to come and stay with us at Broadlands. When Breyani retired to stud, Ingrid sent her here and we went half shares on her yearlings.

The day of the select sale came and Amanda and I got busy with our rinses and glitter as well as all the usual paraphernalia used for the Broadlands yearlings. We felt like we were preparing a couple of film stars! When Kayani, our magnificent grey colt, came into the ring with his tail and mane shining with the silver rinse and the addition of the silver glitter that Amanda had sprinkled on the plaits on his mane and top of his tail there was a hushed silence. Then the arena broke into an uproar of clapping. Of course this beauty topped the sale. There was a similar reaction to our beautiful filly, Stolen Gem. She was a bay, so we had done her mane and tail with a black rinse while green and blue glitter adorned her plaits and tail. She was the top-priced filly of the sale.

Mind you, it wasn't just the horses that looked good. I loved blue, so I always had blue and white scalloped canvas awnings decorating both sides of our yearling alley at the sales. These were nailed along the top of the boxes, and then I used to go out and buy containers filled with flowering plants to decorate the area outside each box.

The yearlings' pedigrees used to be printed in black on blue backgrounds and pinned on the stable doors. The staff were all dressed in blue jeans with pale blue T-shirts with Broadlands printed in large letters on the back; they also had navy blue ones so they could change every day. They all wore pale blue and white knitted caps with pompoms, or depending on their uniforms the navy blue caps.

What with the dogs and my beautiful orange-crested cockatoo, Molly, we used to look like a carnival arriving. Before people got used to my eccentric ways, they used to regard us with a mixture of horror and awe.

I always used to stay at the sales grounds until the last of my yearlings had been collected by their new owners. This was because I found out that a lot of yearlings were not picked up immediately after the sale and that it was sometimes several days or more before the floats would arrive to collect them. Once we even found a dead yearling in its stable. After that I used to go round and inspect all the boxes and open the top doors of those that had been shut. After the sales the studs would depart, leaving the yearlings that had been sold to be collected by the new owners. Basically it was not the stud's responsibility any more. So we used to stay and feed and water all those that were awaiting their transport, sometimes for as much as four or five days. I did bring it up at several meetings, but nothing seemed to get done about it.

* * *

The Joburg sales were always such fun, with a great social gathering as well as some hard-core selling going on. We used to give buffet lunches outside our office in the yard. Under the shade of our big blue umbrellas we would dish out delicious food, all to be washed down with an abundant supply of wine and champagne, as we met up with all our racing friends, prospective customers, trainers and vets.

Whenever we had to go to the Joburg sales, Frank and I used to stay with our great friends, the jockey Tikki Carr and his wife Naomi. They had a spare apartment that they very generously offered to us, since as we always had the dogs and Molly with us, staying in a hotel would have been out of the question.

Tikki and Naomi owned and ran a large scrap metal business. Naomi used to leave early in the morning and always with a large sum of cash, as the business was all conducted with cash sales. One year I told her I thought it was a crazy idea, carrying so much cash around. Almost a year later, I got the terrible news that she had been killed. As she drove up and stopped to get out of the car, she was surrounded by this gang, who shot her and badly wounded the man who had accompanied her – and of course they got away with all the money. It was such a tragedy; she was a lovely and caring person.

One year while we were up in Joburg we were having dinner at a very good restaurant that had a big buffet table. I decided to choose from the buffet and at the end of the table, I saw several objects that looked like lobsters. At first, I thought they must be part of the table decoration, until I touched one of them and its eyes moved. I love lobsters; I had spent so much time swimming with them in the Mediterranean and watching the way they would decorate their caves in the rocks with coloured bits of glass which they had picked off the sea bed or with other colourful objects that had caught their eye. I also loved their courtship dances, holding each other's claws, just like two loving people holding each other's hands. I had a strict rule that nobody ate lobster in my house, and not in restaurants if I was around.

Now the problem was that I could not leave these lobsters in the restaurant to get boiled to death while they screamed with agony. So I spoke to the waiter about buying them and asked if there were any more live ones that I could also buy. He said there were a few in a tank at the back, but he would have to ask his boss. The answer that came back to me was that they could not sell them all as they had to cater to their other clients. Not put off by this, I went to speak to the boss myself and offered him exactly double the price for each of the lobsters in the restaurant. So that evening I landed up with about 20 live lobsters.

The next day I had to go and buy a huge saltwater oxygen tank with rocks and food for my lobsters. I settled them into our office at the sale ground, but one of them did not look well so I asked my great friend Brian Baker the vet if he could help. Brian laughingly said that he knew nothing about lobsters, but would bring his stethoscope and call his office in Durban to see if his secretary could find out something for him. He arrived with another very famous vet, Tim Roberts, who was also a great friend and had heard about my escapade at the restaurant.

It soon got around the sales ground and we had a swarm of vets all wanting to examine the lobsters. They thought it was hilarious. It became the buzz of the sales and everyone was visiting our yard to see the eccentric Pat O'Neill and her latest acquisitions. So we kept them until we could put them back in the sea, as Johannesburg is miles away from the coastline.

This certainly wasn't to be the last lobster rescue mission I embarked upon – years later I discovered that they had started selling live lobsters in my beloved Checkers. There they were in a glass tank in the fish section! I was horrified and bought up the entire stock several times. Then I called up Whitey Basson, the managing director, and explained the issue to him. Thankfully he then gave instructions for Checkers to stop stocking live lobsters and today the tank is full of live and very brightly coloured tropical fish, which are a pleasure to watch.

Another rescue adventure also took place in Johannesburg, though this time it was a dog. Amanda was staying with friends who owned one of the horse transport businesses and next door to them lived a member of the AWB. This was a right-wing Afrikaner group whose leader was the late Eugene Terre'Blanche. Eugene was a very bad rider and used to tear around on a horse with all his followers. Amanda arrived in tears one morning, saying the AWB neighbour had a dog, a cross-Rottweiler that was chained up in his yard, and that he was coming home drunk every night and beating the poor dog up. She had been woken up again the previous night by the dog screaming in pain. She told me she could not bear it any longer and planned to rescue the animal. She cooked up a whole plot but first we had to get special clippers to cut through the chain and also break into his yard. On the morning of our departure, Amanda got up at five o'clock and with the help of her friends rescued the dog, which we called ET after the infamous Eugene Terre'Blanche. Unlike his namesake and previous owner, ET turned out to be a wonderfully amiable animal.

My first dog rescues started soon after Amanda arrived on Broadlands to start work on the farm. I had a lovely Doberman called Lucy (there was a very good song at the time called Lucky Lucinda). Lucy was with my mother most of the time and was in the portrait by the famous artist Von Michaelis of my mother, Lucy and myself holding our stallion Adamastor. When Lucy finally died from old age, I decided to replace her and called Animal Welfare in the nearby town of Gordon's Bay to enquire about whether they had a dog on death row. I was told there were 18, so I said I would take the lot. Poor Amanda had to go to the vet every day for a week to have them spayed and neutered and when they all arrived back in the horse box, Jim had included an extra one. He told me she had been brought in to be put down, so he thought he would just add her to the general collection. She was a divine little black mutt that I named Sammy Joe. That was in 1989. In 2011 we had a grand total of 35 rescued dogs in the house.

I didn't draw any lines when it came to rescuing animals and one day when my friend Sue Snaith called to say a sale we had just returned from was letting all the mares that hadn't reached their reserve go to a butcher, I grabbed Amanda and we flew back to the sale grounds. There I managed to acquire the lot – a rough total of 35 mares! Some to my horror were already at the station being loaded onto the train, so we had to get there as quickly as possible. Two had already been loaded by the time we arrived and I had to do a lot of explaining and showing the sale documents to prove that I had indeed paid for them and they were now mine.

Courier Transport, which was owned by the Cohen family and did all our horse transportations at the time, heard that I had rushed to the rescue of the mares and offered to take them all to my farm free of charge. I did not have enough room on the stud to accommodate all these new mares, so Gurd van Heesch, our neighbour, offered to take some of them, while Shirley Pfeiffer, who owned Arc-en-Ciel, offered to take half; then other people took one or two and I ended up with about 10, one of which was an old mare called Queen of Fortune, who had in her day been a great race filly. Saved from slaughter, several of these mares went on to produce black type winners, including my beloved Queen of Fortune. One stud owner wrote to the newspaper saying he did not know what all the fuss was about; he saw no reason why mares that did not reach their reserve should not go off to the butcher. He saw nothing wrong with that. I did not bother to reply; if that is the kind of mentality some stud owners had, one could only hold them in contempt.

CHAPTER

13

From dogs, cats and horses to lobsters, my rescuing of animals has never stopped. My first baboon rescue started with Buster, a tiny baby who was featured on the front page of the *Argus*. I called up the SPCA and as I had had so much experience with baboons in Kenya I offered to give Buster a home.

Buster arrived in 1981, then a female I called Baloo arrived the following year. I gave them all names starting with B for baboon. They were brought up sleeping in bed at night, with bottles and nappies. I handed the baboons over to Amanda and Belinda, a girl from England who was helping Amanda at the time. Belinda had the baby male in bed with her and Amanda the female. I will never forget one night when we went to a restaurant in Gordon's Bay for dinner. The baboons had come with us, as one could not leave the babies unattended at home. Belinda had a little carrier bag strapped round her waist for Buster which she would then cover with her jersey. At one stage, Buster was getting a bit restless and her jersey started moving. A waiter arrived and nearly dropped the plates. He stared with horror at her moving stomach and said, 'Madam, madam, just hold on a minute! I will quickly call the ambulance; the boss would not like a baby to be born in the restaurant.' Belinda lifted her jersey and showed him the baby baboon, but he was not amused. He called it a horrid little *apie* and went off to inform the boss. The boss was duly produced and, unlike the waiter, accepted the new guest with much amusement and pleasure. Soon there was a crowd around the table all wanting to touch the baby baboon; the children especially were thrilled to be able to lift him up and have him cling to them. One little boy burst into tears when baby Buster was taken from him and begged his Daddy to let him have a baby baboon.

Soon I was collecting a lot of rescued baboon babies. They were all so sweet and adorable and had to sleep cuddled up in bed with me at night as well as clinging to me during the day. I have always found that sharing one's sleep with wild animals makes them much tamer. I think it is the constant bodily contact that gives them the security they lack when they lose their natural parents.

The baboons and the dogs were my constant escorts, sleeping with me at night, accompanying me in the car and following me around the farm. An interesting fact I learned was that when I had to go out without them, the baboons would panic if I left them with the smaller dogs – I had to leave them with a big dog; this clearly was their security.

I had a marvellous dog called Pick Up that I had rescued as a puppy when he was thrown out of a car in front of me. He adored the baby baboons and would lick them, lie next to them at night and act as their constant companion. He grew into a big dog and he was the one that they trusted the most to look after them when I was not around. It was too sweet; whenever I was shopping he would lie on the back seat of the car with four or five baboon babies attached to him; all the other dogs had to find their own space elsewhere in the car.

My lovely Mercedes was always full of dogs, baboons and often Molly the cockatoo as well. It became a well-known sight in the supermarket car park and people would crowd round to stare through the windows at this eclectic collection of animals. Then whoever was the latest baby would have to accompany me while I was doing the shopping or going to Pam's the hairdresser.

I have always done my shopping at the same supermarket – the Somerset West branch of Checkers. In the supermarket I always had to be careful at the till because there was a collection of sweets displayed there and a little hairy hand would reach out and try to grab a handful – much to everyone's amusement. I think the owners of these stores don't always realise what wonderful service some of them provide so I wrote to Whitey Basson and told him how wonderful his Somerset West supermarket was. I got a lovely letter back saying that in future I could have all their waste fruit and vegetables for the animals. Nowadays I also get all their waste meat, which feeds over 60 dogs – ours and the staff dogs; of course I put lots of garlic with it and my brother when he is visiting never stops complaining about the terrible smells emanating from the kitchen every morning. But the dogs all survive into vast old age – I even have two 20-year-old dogs, which is practically unheard of, as well as a fair number in their late teens. All the damaged vegetables and fruit now go to my collection of vervet monkeys and baboons and the really bad stuff goes to the cattle, pigs and goats. I could certainly not carry on feeding all the animals without the help of Checkers and I am immensely grateful for the truckload of food we pick up from them daily.

Not long ago I sent my cook, Amina, to do some shopping for me. She is a big smoker and I had given her an open cheque made out to Checkers, so that the amount of the shopping could be filled in. There are about 14 tills, with queues of people, and when she got to the till, the cashier refused to fill the cheque in until she had called me up to check that she was able to do so. 'Mrs O'Neill never buys cigarettes!' she said. I love that sort of familiarity and how, after so many years, although the world grows larger, a sense of village life can still be retained, where faces and names are recognised and a sense of caring remains.

* * *

Another lovely baboon rescue was Lily, who had already been adopted by some other people who could no longer keep her. She settled in with all the others, who were old enough now not to have to cling to one any more during the daytime, but would follow me everywhere. A film company needed a baboon to do a scene for their film and were put in touch with me. Amanda and I thought Lily would make a great film star, so we set off with her ready to spend the day on set.

Her scene involved running along and climbing in and out of a hedge bordering a footpath by the sea. This scene had to be repeated numerous times until the film crew were satisfied. I would take her down to the hedge and release her and Amanda would stand at the other end with a packet of sweets and bananas. Lily was having a great time, until suddenly she was no longer there – we searched the hedge and she was nowhere to be found until, panicking, we heard raucous laughter coming from the other side of the hedge and rushed over to see Lily reclining in the director's chair. She looked so relaxed, with her legs spread, one arm dangling over the arm rest and the other hand holding her lollipop, while she happily surveyed the film crew who were crowding around her taking photos of their new director!

Another amusing Lily story was when she fell madly in love with one of my lunch guests. By now all the baboons had been enclosed in a large area at the back of the garden. While they had everything they wanted, this was not always to their liking, as they were very sociable animals – and although I had built them their own pool at the back, they were used to swimming in Frank's pool by the house. Somehow they had all broken out while we were having lunch and the lot of them made a wild dash for the swimming pool, which was right next to where we were seated for lunch.

One of my friends, Peter Siddons, who used to visit us often, was sitting there highly amused yet totally nonplussed by the commotion and splashing about in the pool. Peter was used to the baboons, as I had often taken them to lunch at his house when they were still small. That day he had on a very expensive red cashmere jersey and Lily, suddenly recognising her old friend, leapt out of the pool and jumped onto his lap, all the while hugging him around the neck, while the pool water poured from her dripping fur. That lovely jersey was shrinking before our eyes! The other guests were delighted and took lots of photographs of this new lunchtime love affair.

Peter had some of these photos made up as his Christmas cards and he used them for many years. Lily of course would not let him go, so Peter had to carry her back to her enclosure and sit with her until I had got the other ones back in, by which time there was very little left of his jersey.

* * *

In the beginning, before the ongoing urban encroachment around Broadlands, my beloved baboons were never enclosed. Every now and again there was the tinkling sound of an expensive artefact in the house being thrown to the floor. One such time was a true tragedy, when the baboons threw my priceless Tang horse, an ancient Chinese artefact from my stepfather Furness's treasured collection, from its prominent position on top of the cupboard to the floor. What a financial disaster that was!

Another nearly very costly event occurred when I was out to lunch one day. They went rifling through the drawers in my bedroom, took all my lipsticks out and finally got hold of my mother's magnificent three-strand pearl necklace with its huge diamond clasp. For days the staff were following a trail of pearls into the stable yard, but there was no sign of the rest of the necklace or the diamond clasp. Weeks later, Jimmy, Kalu's keeper at the time, finally found them at the bottom of the water tank.

The baboons were, for obvious reasons, better companions when outdoors and would accompany me on my daily walk around the farm. I would check on the fencing and the horses and make a mental list of what needed doing. I always ended my sojourn up by the river, which luckily for me ran through the property. It gushed down from the mountains above us and ran through the top part of the farm, then under the main road, through the bottom farm and out to sea. Thanks to the river, I was able to have three large dams on the farm. One came with the farm when we bought it, another one I built down on the stud side and Frank built the third on the racing side. My dams all had islands in the middle of them for the prolific birdlife as well as any other creature in need of a safe and secluded resting place.

We had a lovely springer spaniel called Cory, named after a famous cricketer. Cory loved swimming and he would take his daily swim in the dam by the stud farm, followed by the older baboons, with the younger ones clinging to his back and having a whale of a time. I would sit and watch them and the resident ducks and geese – it was always such a pleasure to see my animals playing. We would then continue our walk and inspect the fields and the horses; finally we would go down to the river and rest a bit in the shade of the trees, as the river ran through a forest.

One afternoon I was sitting on the river bank watching Buster and Baloo swimming and turning the river rocks over in search of 'dudus' – a Swahili word for bugs. Both baboons were magnificent swimmers as they had been taught by my husband Frank and when they were babies Cory very kindly used to take them for a ride on his back in the dam every day. On this occasion, the soporific sounds of flowing water were interrupted by the distant and repetitive thud of an axe hitting a tree trunk.

I have a particular love of trees, so I quickly got up and charged off in the direction of the sound. Upon seeing the man I shouted to him to stop, telling him this was private property and that the cutting of trees was not allowed. Then, to my amazement and horror, he screamed back at me and came running at me with his axe raised. He was so close I could see the angry spittle coming out of his mouth as he raised his axe as if to chop me in two.

The baboons, who had heard him screaming, rushed up from the river, saw their precious mother was about to be attacked and charged at him. No man can cope with two five-year-old baboons, both with teeth like tusks. He was waving his axe at them, first trying to get at one then the other, but they were tearing him apart.

I realised they would kill him if I did not do something quickly; by this time he was pouring blood and screaming for my help. My only solution was to run as hard as I could away from the scene. Baboons will never let the leader of the troop out of their sight; not only was I the alpha female, but also their very precious mother. They quickly detached themselves from their victim and came tearing after me. My life had now been saved three times, twice by my lioness Tana in Kenya and now by my baboons in South Africa. Wild animals have this highly developed protective instinct for those they love and will readily sacrifice their own lives to save those of their family members. I remain forever indebted to Buster, Baloo and Tana.

Many of the baboons I have rescued have been the babies of mothers who were considered vermin by farmers and were shot or poisoned. Sometimes they would take pity on the babies and through the 'grapevine' they used to end up with me. Baboons are the most wonderful, loving animals and filled with such intelligence and intuition. I have had so many amusing and wonderful experiences with my babies and alas some equally tragic ones.

One was with my beloved Lulu, who was about eight years old at the time and was a large, fully grown baboon. She had been shoved off a high wall by her companion Bingo, a large male, and I had to take her to our local doctor, John Anderson, as she had hurt her back badly. I think that by this time his waiting room was used to me arriving with various baboons. Certainly his lovely receptionist was, as upon seeing us she always hurried us into a separate waiting room off his surgery. I later heard that apparently the people waiting wanted to know why a baboon should get preferential treatment over themselves!

John arrived and was preparing to give Lulu a thorough examination, but while he was looking for his stethoscope I lost my concentration and let Lulu go. Within seconds she had climbed off my lap and was up on the windowsill. She was a curious being and never having seen lattice blinds before, with a tremendous crash she pulled down the lot! I was so embarrassed, but John didn't turn a hair. He just laughed and carried on as if he was used to having his surgery pulled apart.

He then took X-rays which revealed that over time, Lulu's back would deteriorate badly. It was tragic; it got to the stage where she was dragging herself around on her arms and her flesh was getting raw, as no matter how many bandages I put on, she would pull them off. She was constantly crying and was in such pain. During the night as she lay beside me I could hear her little moans as she slept. I soon realised that I could not for my own selfish reasons let her suffering continue and so decided it would be best to put her out of her misery.

I took her to the vet and held her little hand as she lay on the operating table. While they injected the fatal dose into her vein, she never took her eyes off me for a second. It was as if she was saying, 'What are you doing to me?' Like all wild animals, she would have read my emotions, and I was in such despair, with tears streaming down my face. What was even more terrible was that her heart would not stop beating; finally they had to inject her again directly into her heart. It was only when her little hand dropped out of mine that I realised she was gone. My beloved Lulu is buried on the farm and forever remembered.

When I first started caring for baboons at Broadlands I had two very ill baboons who quickly developed very similar symptoms, first blindness and then rapid paralysis. The solution, I thought, might be found at the zoo's veterinary surgery, so I used to do a two-hour round trip to the zoo daily, where they were put on drips and all sorts of medication. Nothing worked however and they both died.

When Bobby, another baboon, developed the same symptoms, I thought enough is enough – and went straight to John Anderson. John was such a brilliant diagnostician and after a brief examination of Bobby, he said, 'It is obvious, your baboon has got tapeworm on the brain; you can tell by his eyes.' I told him that post mortems had been done on the previous two baboons and nothing had showed up. John thought that this was because they had not done a post mortem of the head.

He then broke the sad news to me: 'I am afraid that Bobby will have to be put down to prevent further suffering.' John came out to the farm; if Bobby was to die, I wanted it to be in familiar surroundings, not like with my beloved Lulu who had been put to sleep in the vet's surgery.

I held Bobby in my arms and twice, as John got ready to inject him, Bobby pushed the needle away. I then turned his beautiful head into my neck, so that he could not see what was happening, and ever so slowly he let go of the suffering and of life. John explained to me that as the baboons were running free and following me around the farm with all the dogs and as there were humans defecating in the forests, their hands would then pick up the worms and as they used their hands for eating, without washing them as we do, they were bound to get infected. John recommended that all the animals be de-wormed every three months, a regime we have followed religiously ever since.

While I never had any further deaths because of tapeworm, I did make the decision to enclose the animals not long after this as so-called civilisation was encroaching on my once peaceful farm with the influx of people and houses getting closer and closer each year.

CHAPTER

14

It wasn't only my baboons that John Anderson saved; in fact, I am eternally grateful towards him for saving my own life. The story started in Kenya on one of my yearly visits. That year there were four of us visiting and as Tubby and Aino Block only had three guest rooms, I shared a room with another guest who had a bad dose of flu. Shortly after we arrived on safari I started to develop flu-like symptoms too. I always carried a stash of antibiotics when out in the bush, so was not too worried. Dr Sydney Teperson, who had been my long-term doctor, had regularly put me on Erythromycin when I needed antibiotics and I suffered no bad after-effects. I therefore thought nothing of dosing myself up with this script and hoped I would soon be better.

The reverse took place and within a few days I started feeling truly terrible. I had to crawl on my hands and knees across the tent to get to the toilet and felt extremely weak and faint all the time. Intuition told me to stop the antibiotics at once and while I still felt weak, I certainly started feeling a whole lot better. It was no use complaining and upsetting everybody else's safari, so I used to sit quietly outside my tent, enthralled with the sense of space and freedom that only the African bush can supply and the wildlife that visited our camp daily – while I may have been ill, I felt at home and at peace there on that chair in the middle of the Kenyan bush.

Once I returned to South Africa, I felt much stronger but found I was still prone to fainting fits. I had fainted quite a bit in my youth so I paid it no attention and went about my business. Once I fainted while carrying buckets of food to Buster and his companions. When I came to, I found Buster sitting beside me with my head cradled in his lap and refusing to let any of the others anywhere near me. He was so protective of me!

Not long after this I was in Somerset West with a car full of dogs and baby baboons, as usual, and I suddenly remembered that I needed to go to the local pharmacy. It was a blistering hot day and while Martin's Chemist always had ample shady parking, that Friday the parking bays were full. I cruised round the block a few times hoping to find a newly vacated parking space, but this was not to be. To kill time while I waited, I thought I would go and see John and chat to him about my fainting episodes; if he could diagnose my baboons I had full faith he could do the same with me.

John Anderson's surgery was a lovely old colonial Victorian fretwork bungalow with a veranda and a garden blessed with enormous trees. This was always useful for me as I would generally have at least 10 dogs in the car who needed to wait for me in the shade. Behind the surgery he has a large area that he has converted into an additional waiting room and surgery for the poor who he treats at a minimal price. Whenever I used to park under the trees I saw queues of people sitting and waiting for him. He is so popular and has such a reputation. My staff refuse to see anyone else.

John examined me, then hooked me up to a heart monitoring machine. He then walked over to his phone and made a call. I heard him say, 'I am sending a patient to you. She will have to go straight into intensive care, but pay absolutely no attention to whatever she says to you, as this is serious.'

I said, 'John, whatever are you talking about? There is no way I am going into Intensive Care.'

'Oh, yes you are,' said John, 'I am sending you to Dr Roos at the Medi Clinic right now.'

I replied, 'John, there is no way I am going to the Clinic! It's Friday, and I have a lot to do over the weekend. If I have to go, I will go on Monday.'

John peered out at me over the top of his glasses, 'My dear girl (I was 70-something at the time), I am glad to hear that you are so busy, but I have to point out to you that if you continue to be busy over the weekend, by Monday you will no longer be here to be so busy.'

I gave in and reluctantly returned home, first to dispose of all the dogs and baboons into Shelagh and Amanda's care and then to collect a few things. Anne Boyd, who was staying with us at the time, drove me to the clinic. They met me at the door with a wheelchair, which I refused to use and instead walked into the Intensive Care Unit. Very soon I was in a bed and hooked up to a heart monitoring machine and not long after this the wonderful Dr Roos, a South African heart specialist with a brilliant reputation, came to my bedside. His reputation preceded him: I had heard that he was the first heart specialist in South Africa who was able, if you got to him within three hours of even a massive stroke, to bring you back to normal.

Understandably, I felt very relaxed and confident in the hands of Dr Roos. In fact, years later he saved my husband Frank, who had developed an embolism on the brain when flying from Australia and had passed out at the Broadlands breakfast table the very day after landing. Frank spent three subsequent days in the Medi Clinic and came back to us full of life. Being the ex-Olympian swimming champion he is, he immediately plunged into the depths of the icy swimming pool, no doubt giving his heart an extra-tough test!

The monitor that I was attached to that night kept screaming away and the night staff kept rushing to my side every time the machine made a sound – none of us got much sleep! Dr Roos came early in the morning to explain that he would have to give me shock treatment to get my heart back into a regular rhythm. He also put me on pills for this condition. Everything went well until two years later when I had to go through the whole procedure again.

Over the years I have come to know Dr Roos well, as I have had to go for constant heart check-ups. On the second occasion, when afflicted with the same symptoms, I was once again put into the Intensive Care Unit. He came to see me the following morning and said, 'Pat, I have to tell you that you are an extremely obstinate woman; it took not only one shock to get your bloody heart back into rhythm but two!' He had been to a heart conference in Australia, and suggested that I join a volunteer programme on a new medicine, at no expense to myself. He is such a wonderful man that I look forward to my visits.

As a result of the medicines I am now on, I also have to go for blood tests every month, but to be honest, half the time I forget. At

Dr Dietrich's office in the clinic where I have my blood tests done, everyone has read *A Lion in the Bedroom*, so while I am waiting, they are always asking me about the animals. This, of course, is when they are not complaining about not being able to find a vein. They are all so sweet and funny as they hunt around to bring up one of my old slippery veins to the surface, so as to be able to insert a needle.

This reminds me of another time with the wonderful John Anderson. My great friend Peter Gray, who was a specialist in clinical medicine at Durham University in England, used to come and stay with us every year and on one occasion he had cause to take me to Dr Anderson as I was not feeling well.

I introduced the two of them and told them they had much in common since John, as well as being a great doctor, was also a wonderful musician and a great artist. Peter at one time in his youth used to play the violin in an orchestra. I will never forget how I lay on John's table with a forgotten thermometer stuck in my mouth and suddenly heard the wondrous notes of a popular symphony sound in the room. I was totally forgotten while John and Peter were lost in the music, each playing a violin to perfection. I never stopped teasing them about it afterwards, but I had thoroughly enjoyed every moment.

Sadly, one Saturday afternoon a couple of years ago, all hell broke loose at John's surgery. He was taking care of his last patient and his secretary was about to close up, when an armed gang rushed in. John was thrown to the ground and was kicked and pistol whipped. His assistant very bravely tried to come to his rescue but was also pistol whipped. The secretary then tried to lock herself in her office, but they grabbed her, tearing her blouse, and stripped her of her jewellery and cellphone, all the while with a gun held to her head. Keeping the gun there, they then told her to take them to the safe.

John begged them to leave her and take him instead, so they locked her and the rest of the staff in the bathroom and took him. His hands were bound with a cellphone recharger cord which he had managed to loosen a bit and on the way to the safe he tried to slam a door in their faces, but this brave move failed and he was told to 'kiss the floor'. When he refused to do this they beat him up and emptied the safe of all the staff wages and the day's takings.

In my youth, one never heard of murders or assaults, but now I have had so many friends either beaten up or murdered. My wonderful friend Joan Roots in Kenya was world-renowned, along with her husband Alan, for the animal documentaries they filmed. They were true pioneers of the trade and wanted to show the world the African bush that they felt was quickly vanishing. Very sadly Alan left Joan for another woman and they finally divorced in 1981. She remained alone in their home at Lake Naivasha, which over the years became increasingly dangerous – and particularly for Joan, who was passionate about protecting the area from poachers. I used to visit her often and play with her snakes, porcupines and the myriad other orphaned animals she cared for. Then on 13 January in 2006 she was violently gunned down in her home. It was too tragic for words!

Another great friend who died a very violent death was Campbell Harris, who was the first person involved in tanzanite mining. On this day he was on his way to the mine in Kenya when his Land Rover was stopped and he was shot – what a senseless waste!

* * *

Amanda Shorter was being courted by a very good-looking, tall young man called Craig Carey. He came from one of the farms across the road and he was here almost daily. The baboons utterly adored him and would leap out of the trees screaming with delight when he arrived. He would catch them as they jumped down and swing them around in his arms like beloved children.

As he was so strong he soon became their preferred playmate and they would wait and ambush him as he made his way to the yearling barn in the mornings. I used to tease Amanda about him, saying, 'I see you have got an admirer, but I think he might prefer the primates.' Amanda told me she thought he was much too young for her. To be fair, he was only two years her junior, but who was I to argue! Sadly in 1988 he was conscripted and left to join the army and we all, particularly his primate friends, missed his daily visits to the farm. While he was in the army he started up a long-distance correspondence with Amanda, then in September 1989 his father was tragically killed in a car accident and he was immediately given exemption from the last year of service in order to return home and run his parents' Windsor Stud.

In 1990 Amanda and Craig were happily engaged and in 1993 they had a lovely wedding in the garden here at Broadlands. An enormous white tent was erected, inside which an altar had been placed, and it was here that our beloved priest Father Tom married the couple. Amanda looked radiant in her beautiful white wedding dress. After the wedding, there was an enormous lunch prepared in a large marquee on the croquet court next to the swimming pool. This croquet court always had many uses, one of which was that it made an ideal setting for showing yearlings to visiting guests and prospective buyers. Alvon Collison was hired as the entertainer and he sang a beautiful and most romantic song from *Phantom of the Opera*. As he hit the high note at the end of the song the parrots and peacocks all let out an almighty shriek and together they all finished the song – is was truly marvellous.

Kalu, of course, made all the preparations very difficult as she chased everyone around while they were trying to set up the tables. Thankfully she left us all alone when she discovered that sliding down the marquee was great fun. She could scamper up to the top and slide down the sides – this she did repeatedly with such enjoyment while we all scurried around below getting the venue ready. Thankfully and miraculously by the time the big day dawned we had managed to confine and contain all our beloved primates for the duration of the wedding day.

Amanda had put blue bows on all the dogs, so they added to the glamorous wedding, and to cap it all, as Amanda and Craig faced each other at the altar, the peacocks let out a few deafening cries and drowned out the wedding vows.

Amanda then went to live in Craig's house on his parents' farm and a year later their lovely son Justin was born. Amanda used to come every day to the yearling barn and baby Justin was brought up with all the dogs and the baboons. I was rescuing baby baboons at the time, so they grew up sharing bottles, and as he grew older he was taken for rides on Kalu's back – all, for Justin, the order of the day!

Not only were there baboons about, but we also had rescued caracals and black-backed jackals who also thought they were dogs, running around the house with the rest of the pack. I had built enclosures for them all, but they preferred human companionship, again having been rescued from shot mothers and brought up on bottles. With all the baboons and dogs the jackals had sort of lost their identity. Very sadly, when I had to sell some of the farm when all my money started disappearing, they were killed by one of the new owner's dogs. It was so dreadful seeing all those beloved beautiful animals destroyed because of their trust in humans and dogs.

The caracals eventually died from feline AIDS. At the time I

assumed the one was dying of old age and did not think of taking it to the vet. There were four of them, but when the second
one showed the same symptoms, I summoned the vet, who had to
dart her first in order to diagnose the symptoms. He then told me
they all had feline AIDS. I had neutered the males when they were
young, so at least there were no cubs to carry on this deadly virus.
Once again I had to say goodbye to more of my beloved animals.

* * *

When I first came to South Africa I met Anton Rupert, who at the
time was funding the restoration of the beautiful old houses of
Stellenbosch and, as I later learned, of Graaff-Reinet too, as this
was where he had been brought up. Architecturally, Stellenbosch
has to be one of the most famous towns in South Africa, with all
its magnificent old Cape Dutch buildings, sitting alongside some
lovely old English colonial homes with their detailed fretwork. At
the same time I met Anton's two sons, Johann and Antonij, who
were both so lovely to me – when they came to lunch they walked
around admiring all the old oak trees on the farm, and told me they
needed spraying as they were getting mildew. Having lived most of
my life in France and Kenya, I was not particularly familiar with
oaks, but then the very next day they arrived with several men and
some huge spraying machines and set about supervising the spraying of my beautiful old trees. What a wonderful family!

The other day I had lunch at a lovely little restaurant in Somerset
West called Imibala (meaning colours in isiXhosa). As I arrived I
saw a huge figure of a lion constructed from wire guarding my parking place right at the front door. So many unemployed immigrants

in this country make wonderful animal sculptures from old wire and the lion at Imibala was a perfect example of the wealth of creativity these artists have to offer. The restaurant is owned by Johann Rupert's wife, Gaynor, and all profits go straight to the Imibala Trust, which provides clothing and education to poverty-stricken children and also offers art and computer classes. The art gallery that adjoins the restaurant is run by Leo van Straten and showcases paintings and sculptures by local artists, with profits, again, going straight into the trust.

Gaynor, who was as usual looking radiant with her striking blue eyes and blonde hair, was telling me that she and Johann were to have lunch in the royal box with the Queen at the Royal Ascot meeting. A wonderful story has to do with a brooch that my mother would always wear into the winning enclosure at the races. It became her 'signature' piece, but during one of the times I had to sell some jewellery, I had to send it to Sotheby's to include in an auction that took place at the Vineyard Hotel in Cape Town. Quite by chance it was bought by Gaynor, who told me she would be wearing it to Ascot. I was so touched that my mother's brooch is still worn amongst the horseracing people of this world and I can't think of anyone I would rather have wear it than Gaynor.

L'Ormarins was originally owned by the family of a great friend, Ann Boyd. It now belongs to the Ruperts and is today a renowned wine farm as well as a very famous stud farm called Drakenstein. When I went there I was shown around by the lovely Gaynor, who owns all the horses. The stud is set in the foothills of the Groot Drakenstein Mountains, with a huge waterfall that plunges down the mountainside and feeds the enormous dams, one of which, as the sun sets, shows a complete reflection bathed in pink of the mountain and part of the stud with all its white fencing. The original late-seventeenth-century Cape Dutch farmhouse on the foothills of the mountain is being restored to its former glory. This is a model stud, with beautiful well-kept barns and stables. Seeing the yearlings and Gaynor's lovely new stallion Trippi convinced me that his progeny will set the South African tracks alight. The highlight of my day was seeing another magnificent stallion, Horse Chestnut. I remember him so well from my racing days and having his lovely face nuzzling mine almost reduced me to tears.

Gaynor and Johann Rupert bought the adjoining farm, Bellingham, from the Beck family (the house stayed in the Podlashuk Trust). Graham loved looking over L'Ormarins and seeing the paddocks and horses, and his wife Rhona wanted the farm to be owned by someone who would love and tend to her gardens. It was here that I was given a birthday lunch in 2011 by my dear friend Jeannie Bloch, who had also invited my great friends John Freeman and Chris Mauerberger and a number of other guests. Leon Coetzee, the estate manager, is not only a great gardener but also a fantastic chef, and he cooked us an exquisite meal. Soup, which I love, was followed by salmon with beautiful little bouquets of vegetables on the side. Leon told us of how in November of the previous year he had been viciously attacked in his home. It was about midnight and a disgruntled farm worker who no longer worked on the farm broke into his home and stabbed him 38 times. Left for dead, Leon was having none of it; he managed to crawl 70 metres to the homestead where he set off the alarm. A security company arrived within minutes; thankfully his attacker was caught and jailed for 20 years.

I had a lovely 2012 birthday lunch there with the same friends and my wonderful friend Aino Block, who was visiting at the time. Jeannie arrived at the birthday party covered in bruises as two weeks earlier she had been attacked in her home outside Stellenbosch.

Luckily she was not stabbed. I am hoping that in 2013 we won't have any tales like these to tell!

* * *

After her first marriage Ann Boyd decided to start breeding racehorses. She purchased the now famous Summerhill Stud in KwaZulu-Natal and not long after this she married Brian Boyd. After 20 happy years they sold the farm to a syndicate which included Mike Goss. Today it is the largest stud farm in Africa and breeds magnificent winners. A third of the farm's horses belong to customers as far away as the United States, Australia and Japan, to name just a few. Ann and Brian used to come to Broadlands every year on holiday. After Brian's death Ann still comes down from her home in KwaZulu-Natal and stays for a month or two.

In the early days, Ann, along with many others, was taken by the beauty of Broadlands, which she was very fond of capturing on camera. One of the features of Broadlands was the front entrance gate with its huge white columns, which back then were topped by large sculpted horses' heads I had bought not long after we started the stud. The other features were the very long driveway lined by poplar trees under which I planted thousands of brilliant blue as well as white agapanthus. The whole effect was really quite spectacular. Cars passing on the N2 below used to get a lovely view of the manor house as it sat on a rise, with the magnificent Hottentots Holland Mountains as a backdrop, and the paddocks, with all their white fencing and flowers, as a frame. It became a famous Cape landmark and these days so many people still tell me how they used to love driving by and looking up at the beautiful stately house and wonderful fields full of horses.

One morning Ann was wandering around the front stoep after her early morning swim. With her camera in her hand and a small bikini on, she set about trying to capture a few pictures of the driveway, framed by the white-fenced paddocks with the beautiful mares and foals in the background. The light I believe was just right and she was so busy with her pictures that she never noticed Kalu coming around the corner of the house, followed closely by her keeper Jimmy. Kalu loves to remove people's clothing – and, not one to miss out on a golden opportunity, she quickly stripped Ann of her bikini.

Kalu finally managed to put it on herself and then, thrilled with her new clothes, rushed up onto the roof. In the meantime Ann was bouncing up and down, much I might add to the delight of Jimmy and the gardeners. It is a good thing Ann had such a lovely figure, as she was much more worried about Kalu grabbing her camera than she was about parading naked on the front doorstep with Jimmy, the gardeners and no doubt many others staring at her agog.

Ann standing on the stoep looking like she had just stepped out of a nudist colony is a moment I will never forget. Kalu, when she was up to no good, had a habit of appearing out of the blue behind you and stripping people was one of her favoured activities.

We had a young teenager staying here once and he was just about to plunge into the pool when Kalu appeared around the corner and within seconds had stripped him of his boxer shorts and left this horrified and terribly embarrassed young man trying to cover up his private parts from all the amused onlookers at the nearby lunch table. I could feel his enormous embarrassment, so I quickly went to fetch him a towel. Kalu, on the other hand, was rushing around in his shorts hooting with delight. There was certainly never a dull moment at Broadlands!

CHAPTER

15

Kalu had an outside cage built for her quarantine period, the bedroom door of which was off my office. The outside area went down to the ground underneath; the top section of this was a platform and below the platform was the Broadlands wine cellar, which was in the basement. The wine cellar was well utilised back then. When my mother bought the farm, since half of it was a wine estate we were members of the KWV and allowed to purchase wine at cost price. I used to go to their offices every year and buy a year's supply for the farm – of gin and brandy as well as cases of wine. During the racing season, we always had enormous lunch parties and hosted numerous house guests. So there were endless gins and tonics poured, much wine and champagne consumed and a never-ending supply of brandy to wrap up each and every party.

Kalu, being so clever and an incipient alcoholic, used to watch the staff going down into the cellar and emerging with arms laden full of bottles. She very soon hatched a plan. On one of her excursions, she had found a saw and keeping it hidden had taken it into her sanctuary. One evening after all the staff had left, she managed to dig up a section of her wooden flooring that was over the cellar and make a large enough hole in the concrete part of the ceiling to give her access to the cellar. The next morning we found a very drunk chimpanzee, surrounded by empty bottles and suffering from a massive hangover. It was hilarious really; she was so human, holding her head in agony while sitting by her pond, and with the other hand pouring water over her head with her sponge. Half the morning she just lay or sat there, sponging her head, uninterested in food or loving hugs and kisses; she just wanted to be left alone and kept fending off all attempts to cuddle her. She obviously had a dreadful headache. I tried to give her an aspirin as I had no idea what one did for hangovers, but thought an aspirin might help. She refused to take it and kept pushing away my hand that held the syringe that I wanted to squirt down her throat. I gave her a great kiss and said, 'It bloody well serves you right!'

Kalu usually spent her days accompanied by her keeper Jimmy, running around the farm, except during our lunch period, which we made from noon to three daily. Jimmy would then bring her back at noon and they would stay in her enclosure until lunch was over. Any house guest staying at Broadlands would have to acclimatise to the Broadlands way of living, which meant a very long lunch break. The compensation, of course, was being able to have a holiday in the Cape, with its wonderful climate and lovely beaches right on the doorstep – not to mention, in those days, a luxurious farm with a large staff that catered to your every need. This I know more than made up for the downside of having to put up with a chimpanzee, baboons, dogs, cats and jackals underfoot, as the same wonderful friends returned every year for years on end.

A quite bizarre incident occurred with a lunch guest who was an Arab prince and one who was clearly not too well travelled. He said he would love to see the chimpanzee he had heard so much about, so I took him through to my office to see Kalu, who of course was behind her wire barrier with Jimmy. Kalu had fallen asleep on her mattress and Jimmy was sitting behind the wire mesh, leaning forward, his face resting in his hands as he watched something on the television. The prince approached the cage slowly and, cautiously extending his hand, tickled Jimmy's nose through the mesh, all the while saying, 'Lovely chimp, lovely chimpy.' I was simply too embarrassed to inform him of his mistake and hurried us all out of the room.

Buster and Baloo were by this time enormous fully grown baboons aged about 15 or 16. Kalu had always been a bit nervous of Buster, and while they did have their own enclosure, one day Buster broke out. The first thing the maids did was to lock all the doors and windows, as he was bound to head for his old home in the house. Then the next thing they heard was a frantic pounding on the front door from Kalu's keeper, Jimmy, who in his fear of Buster had deserted Kalu to close himself in the house too. Then just a few seconds later, the doorbell rang and it was Kalu, shaking her fists in fear as she made a beeline for her old sanctuary. Once inside, she closed herself in and leaned heavily against the gate, just in case Buster should try and open her door!

When Buster and Baloo were fully grown they were creating so much damage around the house, breaking the china, raiding my

LEFT: Handsome is as handsome does – for all his looks Free State was not a very successful sire.

BELOW: My magnificent Marysa, one of the greatest fillies I ever trained, if not the greatest.

BOTTOM: Terrance Millard with one of his winners. He and his wife Joyce became great friends of mine.

Marysa

OPPOSITE PAGE:

TOP LEFT: My Lovely, the Cape's champion two-year-old, ridden by our wonderful Garth Puller.

TOP RIGHT: Frank had an eye for a horse – Pat leading one of his winners into the enclosure.

BOTTOM LEFT: Enid leading in Miss Lindeman, who was named after her and who turned out to be the South African champion sprinting filly. Every time she ran she was simply unbeatable.

BOTTOM RIGHT: The perfection of beauty – Swan River, ridden by Harry Cawcutt. Pat is wearing her 'lucky outfit' in this photo.

TOP RIGHT: Marysa.

MIDDLE: Royal Prerogative.

BOTTOM: *Left to right:* Miss International (unconfirmed), Swan River, Naughty Nymph, Highborn Harry, by E Richardson, 1984.

TOP: Swan River, ridden by Garth Puller. No one could fathom why she was so fast and she became the most enchanting spoilt filly that ever raced.

BOTTOM: Miss Lindeman, ridden by Bert Abercrombie, in a clear win, 8 December 1971.

BELOW: Another win for Swan River, ridden by Harry Cawcutt, Natalia Stakes, 9 July 1973. In her two seasons of racing, she was to become famous throughout South Africa and win me 10 races in total.

ABOVE LEFT: Lady Kay, 30 March 1974, at Milnerton – unbeaten in 10 consecutive races.

ABOVE RIGHT: Frank leading in Bejewel, ridden by Patrick McGivern, 28 December 1977, at Kenilworth. She was one of the first fillies brought over from Australia.

ROYAL PREROGATIVE
1969 – 1987
SOUTH AFRICA'S GREATEST STALLION
BROADLAND'S GREATEST ASSET
HE WAS MUCH LOVED.

Lady Kay and Pat at the Broadlands stables. I named her after my mother, whose last title had been Lady Kenmare, because she was, like my mother, so beautiful.

OPPOSITE PAGE, CLOCKWISE FROM TOP:

Mexican Summer ridden by Garth Puller, 27 February 1974, at Kenilworth. Despite his small size, he turned out to be a champion sprinter, winning me 11 races.

Swan River. She constantly acted like a prima donna, almost saying to the crowds as she came into the winner's enclosure, 'Take a good look; you will never see the likes of me again.'

Royal Prerogative's grave. Tragedy struck when the feed companies bought in some contaminated food and my beloved Royal Prerogative was one of the casualties. *(Sam Reinders)*

My Lovely, one of my first Australian fillies.

Royal Prerogative with Pat and Hans. An incredible stallion – 14 times champion brood mare sire, which was unheard of at the time, and he cost me a million pounds.

TOP: Stableyard with ducks. Swan River liked to lean out and keep an eye on all her clucking and crowing friends below as she ate. *(Sam Reinders)*

BOTTOM: Whitewashed walls, expansive green paddocks and grazing horses have always added to the picture-perfect scene of Broadlands. *(Sam Reinders)*

RIGHT: Morgan and Cash, the only rescue dog Pat paid for. *(Sam Reinders)*

BELOW: Morgan at the Animal Care Facility with Cash, Sparky, Ganza and Angel. *(Sam Reinders)*

ABOVE: The Animal Care Facility is not far from Broadlands and the primates enjoy an uninterrupted view down to the azure seas below. Morgan has designed the most beautiful enclosures with tree houses, ropes, rocks and enormous branches for the primates to enjoy. *(Sam Reinders)*

MIDDLE: Michael, Kalu's keeper, outside her bedroom area at Broadlands. *(Sam Reinders)*

BELOW: King Billy of Broadlands awaiting another Marie biscuit! *(Sam Reinders)*

OPPOSITE PAGE: Scenes from the Animal Care Facility and a recent portrait of Kalu. *(Sam Reinders)*

RIGHT, FROM TOP TO BOTTOM: Meet the staff: driver: Hennie Warnick, cooks: Amina Wantza and Magrieta Marwelo, maids: Doris Laubscher and Victoria Witbooi. *(Carmen Nelstein)*

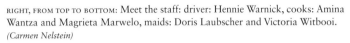

ABOVE: Lunches at Broadlands are famous for roast potatoes, roast chicken, and our special salad dressing! Amina preparing a salad with her constant companion Candice looking on. *(Sam Reinders)*

LEFT: Shelagh McCutcheon would come from Cape Town every morning and ride work for us. She turned out to be an absolute treasure and has been living with us at Broadlands ever since. *(Sam Reinders)*

ABOVE: Editing the book: Donna Cobban and Pat with Nguni (lying) and Mdubi in Pat's office. *(Sam Reinders)*

LEFT: My saviour Chris Myburgh: Kalu insists on inspecting his chest hair.

Both Caryll and I made a habit of raiding the storage rooms under La Fiorentina to furnish our homes. They held lovely antique furniture and paintings ruthlessly turfed out by Rory when he was busy re-doing one of the houses at Cap Ferrat. In my opinion the addition of a dog is always a great improvement! *(Sam Reinders)*

My life in a mural ...

drawers and stealing things, that I decided I would have to build a large enclosure for them. They were like a pair of extremely naughty children, tossing things around and raiding the fridges. As they were both great swimmers, I realised they would have to have a swimming pool to keep them truly happy – and as Frank had taught them to dive, they would need a deep end and diving board too.

When I called up a pool company and said what I needed, the gentlemen asked me how old the children were for whom this pool was required. 'Actually, it is not for any children, it is for three large baboons,' I told him. There was a deathly silence on the other end of the line, then the voice said, 'You are obviously calling from —' then he named a radio talk show that constantly made prank phone calls. 'I am sorry, we cannot help you,' and he put the phone down. So I had to call another company, and having learned my lesson, this time I told them it was for a few rather naughty children who needed a nice safe pool that they could not damage.

While there were many amusing times, there were a few awful moments too. One of them was when Eileen Bestel from Clairwood Stud in Durban was staying with us. She was coming in the front door when Kalu ran up behind her and Eileen, being a bit nervous, slammed the door on her. The front door is over 200 years old and made of very thick oak and is therefore very heavy. In her haste Eileen slammed it on her finger and it took the top of her finger right off. I quickly put it in ice and took her to my beloved Dr Anderson, who sewed it back on again, and he did such a marvellous job that to this day she hardly knows which finger it was.

While some incidents had happy endings, others were less fortunate. Kalu used to take a tremendous fancy to certain people, especially men. We had the famous gardener, Keith Kirsten, to lunch and she fell for the friend he had brought with him. She was sitting on his lap, kissing and hugging him – thankfully, much to his delight. Betty, my sister-in-law, then arrived and as she walked past, made the huge mistake of prodding Kalu in the stomach with her forefinger and saying, 'Don't let her sit on your lap, she is a horrid animal.' Betty had never particularly liked Kalu, who would often go up to her flat and raid her fridge. Kalu, feeling Betty's dislike and objecting to being poked in the stomach, turned around and bit the tip of her index finger off. Right away I put it in ice and she was taken off to a surgeon, but he was not Dr Anderson, who was away at the time, so her recovery was not as successful as Eileen's had been.

Because Betty and her children were living upstairs in the large studio flat on the farm, I realised I could no longer let my beloved Kalu roam the farm freely. Until the incident with Betty, she had never hurt a single soul. She loved everybody and loved getting piggyback rides from the adults, or swinging with the children on the jungle gym that I had set up for them. She also loved giving the children rides on her back through the forest, pretending she was a horse. Amanda always had a flock of the lovely African farm children with her and they of course adored Kalu and the baboons. They loved giving bottles to the baby baboons, or chasing around with the two older ones, Buster and Baloo. There were also two very sweet children who belonged to the Stodels, tenants on the farm. Byron and Chloe were about seven and eight at the time and Buster and Baloo were their shadows when they came home from school. In Kenya, my chimpanzee Joseph was the same: the tiniest child could be entrusted to his care. They would go to the sandpit and play with buckets and spades or use the swing that I had made for my nieces. I used to love watching the happy and intent faces and hearing the childish voices as they sang to him or took him to dance around one of the trees; my own beloved child amongst all these conventional East African children.

Although the primates all enjoyed their freedom so much, it made sense, despite my enormous reluctance, to fence Kalu in. I decided to take one of the big stallion paddocks, which had two large adjoining stables, and I converted the one into a room for Kalu and on the other side I made a bedroom for her keeper Jimmy. I got a Mr Van Heerden to do the job as his company were fencing experts. Kalu was delighted to have so many new-found friends; she even learned to use a hammer and nails and saw wood. They were all fascinated by this chimpanzee helper; when I used to come along there was my beloved chimp, happy as anything, having tea and sandwiches with her new worker friends.

Then the terrible day arrived when the fence was finished. Mr Van Heerden came to me and said, 'I have never had much to do with animals, but this is a human being and we all love her and I feel terrible that I and my men by building this fence are responsible for putting this wonderful creature in prison.' Yet we had to press on with our decision and the vet was summoned to dart her.

Somehow Kalu must have known what was about to happen, for as soon as the vet arrived with the dart gun she grabbed her mattress and held it up against herself for protection. This carried on for several hours, just like a matador holding up his cape. Like the usual coward in these situations, I had fled the scene as I did not want Kalu to associate me with this torture. It was all left to Amanda and when Kalu eventually got darted, she was placed on a stretcher and taken off to her new enclosure while Amanda accompanied her, holding her hand and lying beside her on her new bed while she was still in her half-comatose state.

The next day, I went in to sit with her and she turned her back on me, refusing to have anything to do with me. I was the boss, therefore it was my fault she was imprisoned and she was going to show me exactly what she thought of my treachery. After a few hours, Amanda came and said she would take over. As soon as Amanda came in, Kalu gave a cry of despair and leapt on her back, wrapping her large hairy arms in a stranglehold around her neck. Amanda was six weeks pregnant at the time and feeling ghastly; she was then forced to walk around the enclosure for the next 45 minutes. By the end of this time Amanda was weeping with despair as every time she stopped and tried to unload Kalu, she got a warning grunt and a threat to bite her on the shoulder. Kalu forced her to keep walking. There was nothing anyone could do to help, as Kalu threatened Amanda when anyone came close. Kalu and Amanda were by this time both hysterical. The situation was getting totally out of control and I was terrified that Amanda might have a miscarriage brought on by so much stress and having to carry this enormous weight around for so long. Eventually, I thought to put an open bottle of wine down outside her bedroom. Wonder of wonders, the sight of alcohol worked and Kalu sprang from Amanda's arms onto the bottle of wine.

Jimmy then took the intoxicated Kalu to bed, lying beside her on her mattress, where they spent the night watching the TV that I had installed for her. For the next few nights Jimmy had to sleep there rather than in his own bed. He soon came to me and told me this made life very difficult as Kalu would often wet the mattress during the night, and he was not happy about waking up covered in chimpanzee pee. In addition to this, Jimmy was not able to sleep with his girlfriend, who was complaining that a chimpanzee was getting preference over her.

Over the next few months Kalu slowly got used to her new quarters. She had a large pet pig that I had rescued from the butcher when it was a piglet and had come squealing over to the racing stables. She also had a couple of rescued goats and two bull calves that had also been rescued and had been neutered. When I first saw them they were being chased down the road by a young man with a whip, on the way to the village butcher. So I bought them immediately – I imagine at a far higher price than he would otherwise have got. Kalu loved them all but she especially loved Piggy and she would often lie in the afternoons under the shade of a tree, reading a magazine with her head propped up on Piggy's back.

Kalu was so clever that if I gave her any medicine or vitamins, she would always try them out on Piggy first. If Piggy accepted the syringe full of vitamins or whatever it was, then Kalu would swallow them down herself. Piggy sometimes did not like the taste, and then Kalu would squirt the syringe out onto the floor. While she was settled and happy, it was clear she needed something additional in her diet. Finally, after much trial and error my beloved Dr Anderson suggested I put her on Jungle Vites syrup, which I would mix with a bit of red wine. Kalu used to take the large syringe and, her eyes closed with delight, gently squirt it into her mouth. She would savour every bit and then, once she had finished, hand me back the syringe with a flourish.

* * *

After a few years in her enclosure I noticed that Kalu was getting very thin and not looking well. Tests were done on her and it turned out she had tuberculosis. I was very lucky as my wonderful neighbour, Rosalyn Grobblaar, who owns Monkey Town, arranged for us to take Kalu to the Somerset West Medi Clinic for a chest X-ray. The Medi Clinic staff were most understanding and gave me a protective apron to wear so I could accompany Kalu, who was sedated but still conscious. Like any mother would, I was able to be by her side and hold her hand during the procedure.

In the adjacent inner glass cubicle there were several specialists peering in at us and at the X-ray. Many of them had come out from Cape Town, all fascinated to be able to take X-rays of a chimpanzee. I am told that the chimp is the nearest relative to a human being and is not even one gene removed from a human. If my dearly beloved Kalu is anything to go by, then chimpanzees are a great deal cleverer than a lot of humans I know.

For the next few days Kalu was very sick and weak; she could not even climb to her bed, so we made it up for her on the floor. Luckily, not only did I have the great Dr Anderson on hand, but there was also Dr Bruce Nyland from the Strand Veterinary Hospital to rely on. Dr Anderson put Kalu on human medicine for the treatment of tuberculosis – and as humans have to take a dose every day for six months, he suggested that I keep her on it for nine months, to make doubly sure she was free of it. Dr Bruce Nyland used to come out every evening after surgery and drip her and she was just too weak to protest.

Dr Nyland was also very worried about her surviving; one evening after he had been, I was lying with her in my arms and I thought that she would not last the night, she was so weak. I was desperate, so I prayed hard to God, my father and my mother, as I rocked her precious body in my arms – and suddenly, like a miracle, the moon came out and lit us up in a bright light and I knew my prayers had been answered.

The next day when Dr Nyland came, without knowing what had happened the night before, he said, 'It is like a miracle, Kalu has taken a turn for the better.' The difference in her was unbelievable; although she was still weak, she was up and about and once again taking an interest in everything. From then on she never looked back; today, years later, she is a huge and very healthy chimp who loves and hugs and kisses me every day.

I have had several miracles in my lifetime due to my prayers. One was when I was about 10 years old, living in my stepfather Furness's huge Victorian mansion, with over 100 rooms. I, along with my brother Caryll when he was home from school, my two governesses, and my nanny had our own wing, with our own staff and staircase, dining room and nursery. This was in part due to the fact that my stepfather did not like children coming into the front of the house. My governess at the time was called Miss Unger and she would give me regular beatings, mostly with a horsewhip across my legs. Looking back on it all, I am pleased that she was so strict with me and that I was so disciplined or I would have been impossible.

However, back then when I was still so small, the idea of Miss Unger's whip used to frighten me tremendously. On one occasion, I had done something especially naughty. While I can't remember what it was I did, I do remember that I was going to get a real beating and I was very frightened. Miss Unger's room was next to mine but separated by a double door and I remember getting down on my knees beside the bed and praying to my father to save me. I heard Miss Unger come to the door and stop, but miraculously she never came in and I did not get punished. Before she left us during the war she said to me, 'Pat, I will have to tell you, I never liked you, even though I knew that you used to put your pocket money in my handbag whenever I was ill. I think you should know that the most incredible thing happened to me while we were at Burrough Court. I was coming to your room to punish you and your father stood in front of the door to your room and would not let me through.' I knew exactly the incident she was referring to, as it was the only time as a child I had implored him for his help.

On the subject of miracles, they continued here at Broadlands. One morning I came back from the racing stables at about 8 o'clock and as I walked into my room, my beloved brother Rory was sitting at my dressing table. He had been very good looking in his youth and he was now looking marvellous, with a blue open-necked shirt on and a black sweater. I particularly noticed that the whites of his eyes had that bluish shade that very healthy babies have. I had left him only a few weeks before in France, where he was very ill and emaciated with AIDS, which at that time no one knew much about. I had been with him for three months, spending my time in his room and helping his nurse and lying beside him in bed reading my books. He just loved the feeling of my presence and knowing that someone who loved him was there for him. When I left his side, he used to whisper, 'Pat, come back.'

But by August I had to return to the horses and arrange all the coverings. I arranged to return at the beginning of September and was going to take our marvellous Dr Sydney Teperson with me. Seeing him there in my room at Broadlands, I said to him, 'Rory, you are looking so wonderful!' At the back of my mind, I thought he must have had a face lift. He said, 'Pat, I am feeling wonderful, you do not have to worry about me any more.' We spoke a bit further, then he got up to leave. He was about to shut the bedroom door behind him when he opened it again and put his head round, saying, 'Pat, you do not need to come over, you can call Sydney and tell him that I feel on top of the world and you can both cancel your trip. I love you.'

I also felt absolutely wonderful, so I called Sydney, and his wife Tikki who answered the phone told me he had just left for the hospital. I told her that Rory had been with me and was looking incredible and that he said we did not need to go over to France after all. There was a long silence at the end of the line. Tikki later told me that she had immediately called Sydney and told him that he had better get around to me quickly, as I was delusional. Sydney told her to relax; he thought it must mean that Rory had died, as the same thing had happened to him with another patient.

At 11am I got a call from France to say that Rory had died. It did not worry me and for the next three days I felt as though a current were pulsing through my body, giving me a sense of euphoria. When my brother Caryll called me from South America, where he was at the time, to ask if I had heard the terrible news, I told him I had and that it was all fine.

Caryll had long ago decided that I was a lunatic – in fact his nickname for Broadlands was Broadmoor, after the famous prison in England for the criminally insane – so if he was not convinced of my madness before, he was now certain. 'How can you sound so happy? I thought you loved your brother,' he asked.

Rory's death did not affect me at the time; I was on my cloud nine for about a week and it was only afterwards, when the memory of him looking so well started to fade, that I missed him so dreadfully. He had been such an enormous part of my life and such an incredible brother to me. Even now, as I write about him, I can't help but cry. I have so many wonderful memories. He had hoped one day to build himself a house on this farm and wanted to spend six months a year with me. How I love and miss him!

CHAPTER

16

While Rory's death was by no means easy to cope with, it was my wonderful mother's death in 1975 that will for ever be the worst experience of my life. Rory was still alive then and was with us at the time, as was my brother Caryll.

Mummy had a very bad hiatus hernia, which the doctors, due to her age, did not want to risk operating on. When the hernia's symptoms were severe, she would be in absolute agony and we would call on Dr Teperson to come and give her some pain relief, which involved literally putting her out for a few days. She used to hear this and would beg me not to let him do this to her as it involved her losing consciousness – something she absolutely hated. As I understood it, this was the only way that the colon would then relax and untwist itself.

This went on for about a year, during which time there were about three of these acute episodes. I used to stay with her, lying beside her so that when she was put out I would be holding her hand and be there for her when she came around. Then she got pneumonia and Sydney employed a charming nurse to look after her, but nothing stopped my mother. I came into the room one morning and there she was up a ladder, looking desperately for her beloved meerkat. She was frantic because the meerkat rarely left her side and used to sleep with her at night, curled up beside either her or one of her poodles.

It was several months before she got really weak and could not leave her bed. Sydney warned us all that she did not have long to live, but I simply could not believe that she would not recover. I spent each night sleeping beside her. Sydney, who adored her, got cold feet and instead of his daily visits, his partner used to come. I think he wanted to avoid the emotions that came with watching a dear and beloved friend fade away.

One morning she woke, turned away from me and half sat up in bed. Looking to the right-hand side of the room, her beautiful face lit up and she whispered, 'Oh mother,' as she stretched out her arms in the same direction; she then lay back down and died.

I cannot say that I remember the funeral or anything else too well. Rory took her ashes back to Fiorentina, where he built a large tombstone in the garden on the point of St Jean Cap Ferrat, and when he moved to Menerbes he took her ashes with him and built another tombstone in his beautiful garden there. On Rory's death, Caryll took the ashes and had them buried in the churchyard of the church next to his house at Blechington. Mummy and Rory are now together again. I had the most beautiful stained-glass window built in Somerset West for the church at Blechington, which I dedicated to my mother and which depicted her surrounded by her parrots and beloved animals.

My life changed dramatically after Mummy died. Everything just started to go from bad to worse. Finally in the year 2000 we were forced to start selling off parts of my wonderful farm in order to survive.

It had all started long before, but it took us all so long to realise what was happening. We had been in Broadlands about a year when one day as I was coming down the front steps a very grand car swept up the front driveway and parked under the oak trees. A large gentleman, with shirtsleeves rolled up, turned down the window and said to me, 'Are you the red countess?' Apparently this was a nickname I had been given because South Africa was very much in the apartheid era at the time and to the horror of everyone I had proudly announced at a recent lunch party how much I admired our president in Kenya, Jomo Kenyatta, how proud I was to be able to call him a friend, that I loved the Africans and how good they had always been to me.

Red countess or no red countess, he was clearly set on approaching me. He was very tall and his stomach fell right over his trousers, which he struggled to keep up. All I could think was that if my stepfather Furness had been there, he would have been sent round to the back entrance. When we had known him some time, he took one of my mother's lady friends to dinner at a restaurant in the village, and at breakfast the next morning she laughingly told us how, when they had finished the meal and had got up to leave, his trousers had dropped to the ground and she had to grab them and pull them up and then cling onto them in case they fell again before she could get him out of the dining room.

Extending his hand, he said, 'I am Ward Gant. I would very much like to have a meeting with your mother, as I have some very important issues I need to discuss with you three ladies.' By this he meant my mother, me and my mother's young secretary, Julia.

At that time, I was busy adding an extra wing on to the house. My mother had insisted that the existing house was much too small and had told me to go ahead and build a respectable-sized house.

When she first came to South Africa, Mummy had been advised by her friends in the Jockey Club to use a certain gentleman, a steward of the Jockey Club who was retired, as her financial adviser. All her life, Mummy had been fortunate enough to have someone she could trust and rely on to handle her affairs. The friends at the Jockey Club then introduced her to this gentleman and he and his wife soon became her great friends.

Ward Gant, who was now comfortably squeezed into one of our office chairs, addressed the three of us and said, 'Ladies, I have been watching you all over the last year and all the building and improvements you are doing to Broadlands – might I add at great expense! I feel I cannot sit by any longer and have it on my conscience that I have not taken any steps to warn you of what is going on. Firstly, your accountant is running false wage books with the amount of people you employ. Secondly, he is also making 50 per cent on all the building materials you are buying and in short is making a lovely profit while you are paying double for the materials.' He then recommended a young trainee accountant to take over our affairs and promised to keep an eye on things for us. Mummy found a tactful way of terminating her agreement with the member of the Jockey Club, although they still remained friends. I think the excuse she used was that he lived too far away and she needed someone who could come to Broadlands daily and be on hand when needed.

Julia soon told Mummy that she could not get over the difference in the weekly wage bills and household and building accounts. Mummy's idea of financial management was just to sign the cheques put in front of her. This was sadly an unfortunate failing that I inherited from her and it would ultimately cost me the farm. We saw a lot of Ward Gant; he had a beautiful farm at the top of Somerset West going up the Helderberg, which is now the Erinvale Estate Hotel and Spa, which his family owned and developed many years ago. He also had many factories in an area known today as the Gant Centre.

After my mother died I inherited this enormous farm and all the magnificent horses but the actual money that my mother left me was tied up in various trusts around the world and it took some time to get it all sorted out. Meanwhile Broadlands needed to cover its daily running costs, so our accountant, the same one Ward had introduced us to, said he had a friend who dealt in jewellery and suggested that he give my mother's jewellery to her to sell, so as to tide us over.

I received £18 000 for Mummy's wonderful collection of jewellery, except for a few pieces that I had given to my nieces. I had kept her famous ring, which she always wore and which I now wear, and her pearl necklace. I had also kept an emerald and diamond brooch which was particularly precious. Later, when my finances continued to be difficult, my sister-in-law, Betty, who was a brilliant businesswoman, said, 'Pat, I am going to Europe, let me take that brooch and I will see what I can do.' Betty, who was a great one for bargaining, first took it to England, where she was offered a very good price, so Betty being Betty, she decided to take it to Switzerland and see what she could get for it there. Eventually she sold it for £120 000. I was sick at the thought of having sold most of my mother's jewellery for a mere £18 000, all because our accountant's friend must have known precious little about the value of those pieces.

Another disaster over my mother's jewellery came several years later. I had kept another of her many rings, a colossal yellow sapphire which was so huge and so heavy it was difficult to wear. It was about an inch long and half an inch thick and I had left it with our accountant to put in his safe in Cape Town, as I had had it cleaned with the intention of taking it to Kenya to wear while I was in Nairobi. A couple of days before leaving I asked the accountant to bring it out, and he sort of hemmed and hawed and did not produce it. The next year, before my yearly visit, I asked him the week before leaving to please not forget to bring me my ring. He looked a bit odd and then told me that we had needed the money and he had therefore sold it for R10 000. I imagine its true value was three or four times that amount.

During my mother's lifetime, I had never handled money. I was very spoilt and whatever I wanted I got – thank goodness I had never really wanted anything for myself, as everything in life was for my precious animals. I was in my fifties when my mother died and I gave the accountant my power of attorney. He was left in charge of everything.

Twenty years later, Theodore Goddard, the large law firm in London which had always handled my mother's money, called up my brother Caryll to inform him that they were very worried as the trust money my mother had left me was almost gone. Caryll flew over at once and asked to see the balance sheets and the cash books. None had been kept and I believe the accountant did not even have a proper degree in accountancy. Caryll sacked him on the spot and put Price Waterhouse in charge. One of their directors sent an accountant and a secretary to the farm to try and find out what had happened to all the money. They lived here on the farm for three months trying to sort things out.

So much was to be blamed on my own stupidity. Tubby Block,

my great friend and a brilliant businessman, had warned me about that accountant; Betty had also employed him for a few months before getting rid of him. Both she and another friend, Ingrid Lubbe, also warned me about him, yet I paid no attention to either of them. So did Fred Herter, a friend and top cancer surgeon in America. He had married my friend Solange and they would often come to stay at Broadlands. Yet I still paid no attention – my involvement was with the farm and the horses, not the finances.

I blame myself for letting all my money be squandered away, never paying attention to accounts, trusting everyone and going around in a state of euphoria over the horses and the animals and my lovely life on my beautiful farm. One of the directors of Price Waterhouse felt so sorry for me that he said he would take over my accounts himself and charge me a nominal fee, which he did. He was such a lovely man, but when he died, Price Waterhouse took over the accounting and they were so expensive that I could not afford their services for very long.

* * *

Between my sweet husband, Frank and me, we were an awful pair when it came to money. Frank, like me, had been pandered to from an early age, largely due to his swimming successes. While he had no financial training, when he retired from competitive swimming he opened the Frank O'Neill Olympic Pools in Australia. His two partners handled the financial side of things and made a fortune for him and for themselves.

Frank was the soul of generosity; he bought a lovely big house at Manly for his mother and added on a large separate cottage for his eldest sister Meg, with of course one of his enormous signature pools separating the cottage from the house. He bought himself a magnificent two-storey house with another huge pool and steps going down to the beach at Manly, and bought wonderful paintings from his sister Betty, who had opened an art gallery in Sydney – the paintings were worth a fortune as many top Australian artists exhibited there. Betty had a brilliant eye for art and colour; years later she made a fortune in South Africa with her exotic shops called Bettina. Here she sold wonderful Indian materials, artefacts and clothes. She started out with a small shop on the farm and it got so huge that she eventually had factories in both Cape Town and Somerset West.

One day Frank announced that he had decided to start up O'Neill pools in South Africa. For once I used what little I have of a brain and advised him to use the money to buy land in Australia. I even suggested my Uncle Grant's property, as he had just died and it was coming onto the market at Rose Bay, a big house with a garden going down to the sea. It was later sold for millions. Frank got on his high horse and said, 'Don't start telling me what to do with my money.' So he ended up with large showrooms in Johannesburg displaying various types of pools and an office to which he never went. This was left in the hands of a young manager. Pools were opened up in Cape Town and Somerset West. Once everything was up and running, Frank left everything in the hands of various managers, as, like me, he had never had anything to do with accounts or money in his life. Instead he spent his time on the golf course, where he was at one time a scratch golfer, and when he wasn't playing golf he indulged in his other big interest – horse racing. After a few years, it all came crashing down around his head. The only branch doing well was the one in Somerset West, which was managed by a lovely young coloured man. When it all went bust Frank gave him the business as a present and it is still running today as Clark's Pools.

Frank then took what was left of his money and invested it in the bottom part of the farm, where the vineyards had once been. A small river separated this area from the racing stables and he turned this area into a large grass farm. He bought a bulldozer and built a lovely dam in order to keep the grass farm watered. I insisted that he make a big island in the middle for all the wild ducks and geese, and we used to row out there once in a while. This lasted a few years, but with no interest in the financial side, this eventually went bang too and we had to sell his various trucks and machinery and I paid off the balance of the debt.

Price Waterhouse also informed me that I could no longer afford to keep the racing stable next to Frank's grass farm going and they suggested I sell off the bottom farm altogether. So my beautiful racing stable and all the land over the other side of the N2 highway were sold – to a construction company, of all things! The fillies and colts that were still there were brought up to the stud section – but I had no Royal Prerogative or Averof to bring in a nice yearly income. Averof had died; he had just covered a mare and was on his way to his paddock when he keeled over and died of heart failure. Now, with the lack of finances, each month became a struggle, what with all the staff wages, the animals and the running of the house.

An interesting incident during this time was when I got a crossed telephone line and heard a very interesting discussion with a bookmaker who was demanding payment for gambling debts from his client. I heard the client answer that 'the Royal Prerogative payments' would be coming in at the end of the month – R250 000, I think, was the sum mentioned – and that he could then pay the bookmaker in full. I rushed to our accountant with this news and told him what the profit from the Royal Prerogative coverings should be, but he said that there were no profits and that he was not the one keeping the Royal Prerogative books.

When I could no longer afford Price Waterhouse, the manager of my bank in Somerset West suggested that I get hold of a very good accountant who had just retired and was working from home. Lionel Wasserfall came highly recommended – and what a blessing he turned out to be. He insisted I keep a running account of expenditure on my computer. Every cheque I signed had to be entered on it for the amount paid and what it was for. I also had to keep a meticulous cash book for anything paid in cash, and again the amount and what it was for had to be entered onto my monthly spreadsheet. At the end of the month this record would be handed to him along with wages and income from rental.

What a difference this has made to my life, although it takes me a good four days at the end of the month to do all the entries. I can now see how much the house costs, with the chimp, the cats, dogs and other primates as well as all my beloved staff. Sadly, Lionel came into my life too late, as I had had to sell the farm by then, but thankfully my brother Caryll has made him one of the trustees for what is left.

I had two wonderful friends renting one of the houses on the farm. One of them owned a large framing factory and I had always been under the impression that this was a prosperous business. He came to me one day and suggested that, as I was having a hard time of it financially, to help me out he could arrange with his bank to take a mortgage out on the farm. He would pay the interest every month. He told me this would help us both. I did not understand all his reasons, but at the time it sounded like a wonderful deal to me. The bank arranged all the paperwork and I went in and signed various documents that they put before me. What neither the bank nor my supposed friends informed me was that they were trading in their own bankruptcy and that they already owed the bank R700 000. Being such a trusting person and believing these friends did truly have my best interests at heart, I had not asked anyone's advice before I put my signature to all these documents. After four months, they declared themselves bankrupt and departed the farm in a great hurry. So there I was, unbelievably living on a farm I no longer owned, with a huge monthly mortgage owing to the bank. It was too much to comprehend – and for once it had as much to do with my own stupidity as with other people's greed and the subsequent disregard of the pain they may cause others in this pursuit.

In addition to the enormous mortgage they left me with, I was also left with over R200 000 worth of damage to the house they had stayed in. This had once been a beautiful old barn that I had done up into a two-storey house with a lovely wooden staircase as the centrepiece. The place was once spectacular and had been featured in a leading glossy magazine. While living there these two friends had torn down the wonderful staircase and replaced it with a huge concrete one. In the large main bedroom, they had pulled one wall down in order to build a fireplace and when they left the place was an utter shambles.

Having at this stage lost everything, I was saved at the last minute when Jim Antrobus informed my wonderful friend Graham Beck about the financial disaster that had taken place. Graham and Rhona Beck, the saints that they were, immediately stepped in and paid the monthly interest, thus preventing the farm from being seized by the bank.

John Kalmanson and Shelia Southey, who owned part of Varsfontein Stud, stepped in and gave me R500 000 for my living expenses and the running costs of the farm. This showed me that no matter how many sharks are lurking about, there are an equal number of angels waiting in the wings to add to the goodness of the world. Never have I been more grateful for the tender kindness of friends than at that time in my life.

* * *

We plodded along and although we had some money I knew in my heart that we would one day have to sell the farm. We had a Swiss German neighbour at the time who seemed interested, but before anything had been concluded he would open the front doors and march through our home like he had always lived there: it was quite dreadful – and to make matters even worse he would take catapult shots at my beloved baboons. I was getting dreadfully worried that he might be our only option of a potential buyer when along came the most wonderful couple called the Van der Westhuizens, who in partnership with two businesses, Kine Holmes and Spearhead, bought the farm in 2006.

The Van der Westhuizens were great animal lovers and rebuilt the lovely eighteenth-century barn. I was delighted at this and immensely pleased that they loved all the animals too. I could no longer afford to keep my horses, so I gave them all away. Shelagh, who had taken over the stud section of the farm, had about 40 horses and ran it as a business until the new owners decided in 2010 that they wanted it for themselves. Shelagh had been great with the horses, the mares, foals and yearlings, all of which looked fantastic – but without the proper infrastructure in place, the maintenance of the paddocks was difficult and so gradually the weeds took over. In addition to this they were not fertilised or watered regularly, so little by little, the wonderful grass camps that once stretched out in front of the homestead started disappearing.

Unfortunately the new owners did not know about stud farming either, so things went from bad to worse once they took over the stud business from Shelagh. They also run a scrapyard and part of the historic stable yards is today full of junk; even a broken-down bulldozer decorates the main yard. What I find especially sad is that my precious Royal Prerogative's grave, around which I had once grown a low flowering hedge in the shape of a horseshoe, has been removed. Today there is just the big engraved tombstone and lots of old cars parked there. As one vet recently said, 'One has to close one's eyes when one comes to Broadlands nowadays.'

The lovely eighteenth-century stable yard with the famous silos that one year appeared on the cover of all the South African school exercise books is now, apart from a few stables, part of the scrapyard. The main house and the immediate garden are still beautiful, as I live here. But at my age I am not that active any longer and having hurt my back I cannot spend much time in the huge garden that at one time was included in David Hicks' book *Gardens of the World*.

Along with the purchase of the farm by the Van der Westhuizens came an agreement giving my animals and me the right to live on the farm for the rest of my life. The contract was put together by my lawyer, Abe Swersky, and an additional clause allowed for a three-month window period for all the animals to be relocated following my death. Although legally that contract remains valid, the benevolent feeling towards my animals has subsided over the years. Sadly, what was once a beautiful property has diminished in quality and today my once beautiful and world-famous farm is an eyesore, making me wonder if there was any sense in my signing a lifetime right to live here.

CHAPTER

17

In 2004 an unlikely stroke of luck came my way, along with some angelic friends assisting me, and my first book, *A Lion in the Bedroom*, was published by Media Press in Australia.

Again it felt as if the heavens were looking after me. Betty, my sister-in-law, had brought some great friends, John Alexander and his wife, to lunch. John had been here before and had written a story about me in an Australian newspaper. After lunch, he said to me, 'Pat, tell my family the story of your lion Tana.' I love telling people about Tana and when I finished the story I mentioned that I had written a book about my life but so far I had not managed to find a publisher.

Just like that, John turned to me, full of enthusiasm, and said, 'I'll get it published!' I could not believe my luck. He gave my book to Media 21 Publishing, which was run by Craig Osment and was also part of the Packer Press. This resulted in a lovely young lady called Shelley Gare arriving for two weeks to do the editing. In fact, there was so much work to be done that she stayed an extra week. I had written several chapters on the lives of many famous people I had met through the years, but she discarded these, telling me, 'Pat, this book is about your life, not anyone else's.'

Craig Osment then arranged for me to go to Australia for the book launch. I cannot tell you how wonderfully he and Stephen Balme looked after me. I was flown out at the expense of Media Publishing. Betty was going to come with me, but she had recently been diagnosed with cancer and with all the chemotherapy, she was not feeling well: a week before we were due to leave, she realised she could not make it. Travelling alone was not an option due to my heart condition, but luckily I am so blessed with wonderful friends that one of them came to my rescue at the final hour. My friend Elizabeth Wilson called up another good friend, John Freeman, who was at that time down on Gary Player's stud farm in Colesburg.

Liz said, 'I am so worried about Pat, her sister-in-law Betty is too ill to go with her to Australia and I do not see how Pat will be able to cope with all the airports and the long-distance flights on her own.' Without a moment's hesitation, John agreed to accompany me and quickly left Colesburg for Johannesburg in order to get his visa and travel arrangements sorted out. He then went to great lengths to get seated next to me on the plane – all at vast expense to himself. I now had to have a wheelchair to get across the airport, which at first I found most embarrassing, but I very soon got used to it and it did make travelling so much easier.

Luckily, Media Publishing also managed to get John a booking in the same charming hotel, the Sir Stanford in Double Bay in Sydney. I had a spacious room with a balcony, so was able to feed all the beautiful birds. They had arranged lots of television interviews and I was a bit nervous at first, but everyone was so nice and easy to talk to that I soon got used to all the media attention. The lunches and dinners and signing of books were quite an adventure, not to mention the wonderful free hairdressing they organised for me.

One of the highlights of the trip was being a guest of honour at the incredible Taronga Zoo. I also enjoyed a lovely lunch with Gai Waterhouse and her family and I got to see Tommy Smith's wife Valerie again, who was still looking as lovely as ever. I also went to the races and reconnected with my old hero Percy Sykes. I had seen quite a bit of his ex-wife Cecil Sykes over the years, as she was a great friend of Betty's, and on one of her visits to Broadlands she had bought a lovely house on the outskirts of Cape Town.

From Sydney, I flew to Auckland, New Zealand, for 10 days, for the New Zealand leg of the book launch. Here I stayed with Shelagh's niece Joanne Pannell and her partner, who were marvellous to me. They had such a beautiful home and what was even more wonderful was its location – right next door to the zoo! I would awaken in the morning to the glorious sound of lions roaring and I would close my eyes and pretend that I was back in Kenya with my beloved Tana. I was also guest of honour at the Auckland Zoo and was given a lunch by the director, Guy Cooper, and his wife Jeanette. The place was so beautifully run, with such happy animals all housed within wonderful enclosures. Everyone in New Zealand was wonderful to me, just as they had been in Australia. That last visit to those two countries and the wonderful people I met is something I will never forget.

Media Publishing paid me a dollar a book and the first edition in

Australia sold 25 000 copies, while 10 000 copies were sold in New Zealand. A reprint was then done in both countries. The success of the book kept me going for another year and gave me some extra time to sell the farm.

* * *

In 2006, a friend of Shelagh's sent her nephew, Morgan Bricknell, to Broadlands – and what a stroke of luck that was for us all. Morgan adored animals and his aunt thought the farm might be a good place for him to be. Morgan was born in Johannesburg and throughout his childhood the family moved every year, due to the nature of his father's work. Very sadly his father committed suicide when Morgan was just seven years old.

Morgan grew up under the care of his mother and stepfather and was a rebellious teenager. He was not shy of hard work, however; he took on the cleaning of chickens at KFC and worked in retail stores and waitered. He then started studying graphic design, but his love of a good party meant he was soon booted out of college.

Morgan's grandfather, Aubery Amryss Bricknell, had set aside a significant amount of money which Morgan inherited when he reached the age of 21 and with this he headed to New York city, where he lived for a year, painting (Morgan is a brilliant artist) and partying and meeting wonderful people – until the money ran out and he had to return home penniless.

Back in Cape Town, he worked as a waiter and was very good at this, earning good money in several of the city's top restaurants. When he wasn't waitering he was modelling part-time, but most of his earnings went on clothes, partying, nightclubs and having a good time. However, this kind of life cannot go on for ever and with his aunt's persuasion he arrived at Broadlands. Much to his own surprise as well as ours, he stayed.

One would think that for a very good-looking young man to be isolated on a farm with two old ladies for company would not be much of a life, but Morgan adores all the various animals and they adore him. All the staff think he is wonderful and he spends his life buying them presents – mostly packets of cigarettes, of which I do not approve! Then all my bloody baboons that I brought up in bed with bottles and nappies only had to take one look at Morgan and I was instantly forgotten! Morgan loves to sit in the sun with them while they patiently groom him and he in turn, returns the favour. If I see this I always tease him, saying, 'I hope you don't get too conceited, as they are only looking for fleas: you are obviously covered in them.'

Kalu, like the baboons, adores Morgan. Not long ago I was complaining that her teeth were getting discoloured, so Morgan took his toothpaste and an old toothbrush and showed her how to clean her teeth by doing it several times to his own teeth. She sat very still in front of him watching intently and when he handed over the toothbrush and paste, she had already assimilated the procedure and copied him exactly. He came back astounded and so impressed by her intelligence, something I have known for years.

Another of Kalu's great acts comes from watching television. In one camp she had two wooden tree houses on very high poles, where she could lie during the day in the shade and watch all the activities on the farm. I decided to put a very strong thick rope from one house to another, so that she could go hand over fist between her two houses without having to climb down and walk. She loved this, and then one day, to my absolute amazement, I saw her walking upright on the rope and balancing with a stick. I asked

Jimmy, her keeper, where on earth she had got that idea and he told me that the previous night they had both watched a circus act on the television. Now the brilliant Kalu was copying the tightrope artists – this became one of her favourite pastimes.

Another fascinating thing about Kalu is her ability to sulk. If I have done something that she does not approve of, she will sit and sulk, turn her back on me and stay hunched up, picking her nose. I then have to work out what I might have done to upset her and make amends. The other day, for instance, it took two days before she would even come near me. None of the usual hugs, kisses and grooming and her little baby noises as I smother that adorable face in kisses. I always have to finish before leaving, by making large blowing sounds around her nose; she loves that and chuckles with delight.

It took me a long time to work out why, but I finally realised that the day before the sulk began, Morgan had shut her out of her top field with all the trees, as he wanted to water it. He had to close her in her bottom camp with the goats while the huge sprinklers were on. After she got bored with rounding up the goats, she had retired to her room and spent the rest of the day lying on her back on the mattress, her legs crossed, while she studied the magazines he had given her. Then when she got bored with that she just lay there staring at the ceiling and picking her nose. Morgan of course was not blamed, but instead I was – her horrible mother!

Kalu's daily diet consists of yoghurt, four bananas and cooked potatoes twice daily, a peanut butter sandwich in the morning, along with half an iceberg lettuce in both the morning and afternoon. She also has an apple twice daily as well as a mango, peaches, melon, grapes, litchis and dates. Then just to make sure she is getting all she needs we give her the multivitamins that John Anderson put her on when she was recovering from tuberculosis. I put them in a syringe and she gives them to herself as the syrup is quite tasty. The worm pills are a little harder, so I break the rules here and crush them up in a little red wine. The wine fools her and down the worm tablets go!

When the weather gets hot Morgan gives Kalu and all the baboons empty lemonade and soda bottles that he breaks in half and fills with ice cubes. Kalu loves taking the ice cubes out and sucking them and if there are any left over she rubs these over her face and head. During her evening feed she is very particular and eats everything in order of preference: first she has the yoghurt followed by the fruit, which is also eaten in order of preference – bananas first, followed by pawpaw and then mango and finally her juice, which is also given to her in an old plastic soda bottle. One day, knowing how scarce these were becoming, as Morgan needed them for his ice-cube servings, I thought to ask her for the bottle back. 'Kalu, give me back the bottle,' I said, and without a moment's hesitation she handed me back the bottle. Totally amazed, I then said, 'Bring me the top.' She had earlier unscrewed the top and thrown it on the ground. Once again, without hesitation, she looked about in the grass, found the top and handed it back to me. Morgan and I stood together marvelling at her capacity to understand these basic instructions.

Her juice bottle comes in handy not only for ice cubes and juice but also for soliciting a bit of red wine on the sly. We had some visitors from the United States and just before lunch was served Morgan escorted the guests up to Kalu's enclosure. One of the young men had a glass of red wine in his hand and upon seeing her favourite drink, Kalu held out her arm and beckoned for him to come closer. Then quickly realising that she was getting nowhere fast, she ran and picked up her empty fruit juice bottle and held it out to him, imploring him to put the wine into it. Morgan, taking pity on her, took the bottle and poured the guest's last dash of wine into it. Kalu was delighted, while I was a little furious with Morgan.

Perhaps Kalu's love of Morgan stems from one of their initial encounters. Not long after he arrived to stay at Broadlands, Kalu thought this lovely, tall, good-looking young man was worthy of her affections and she used to constantly beckon him to join her. Morgan wanted to go and sit with her, so I said to him, 'Just remember that she is after all a wild animal, and no matter how loving and human she is, she does not really know you, so don't take anything from her; if she goes through your pockets and finds sweets or anything let her have them; don't grab them back, or she will bite you. Just put your hand out and ask her to give it back.' I left him sitting on a log under one of her trees and she was happily grooming him, kissing him and poking her finger up his nose. She was also very interested in his teeth and kept opening his mouth to take a look. Morgan seemed perfectly happy and so I left them to it.

Kalu then pulled his top off, so that she could groom his back, and when she finally got bored with that, she removed the very expensive belt that was holding his shorts up and put it round her own waist. Much to Morgan's amusement she pranced around for a bit, showing off her new look. In the meantime, some of the staff had collected to watch her antics. She soon returned to Morgan, loving and kissing him all over again. Then, much to all the onlookers' amusement, as Morgan started to move away, she came up behind him and stripped him of his shorts, then to Morgan's horror and embarrassment she took hold of his private parts. Remembering my instructions to never take anything away, or she will bite, he held himself very still while Kalu inspected his manhood, but his terror increased as she started giving her lovely new toy an up close and personal inspection. By this time, practically the whole farm had gathered at the fence, faces pressed against the latticed wire as they strained for a better view of the proceedings.

Poor Morgan was stark naked, with Kalu holding his member in a firm and steady grip as she gradually led him towards the gate. Morgan in the meantime was begging anyone in the gathered crowd to intervene and try to distract Kalu so that he and his manhood could make a daring escape. Thank goodness, the wonderful Hennie Warnick who works on the farm and is our driver was in the crowd. His quick thinking gave Morgan the chance to escape as he lit up a cigarette and passed it through the fence to Kalu. She has a passion for smoking, which I do not permit, although obviously she must have been well versed in the art from her earlier life as she always stubs her cigarette out once it is finished. Now she appeared quite torn in her decision between this fascinating new toy attached to Morgan's body and the glowing ember of a cigarette. Morgan will be forever grateful that after much deliberation, the cigarette won and he was able to make a quick escape, snatching up his belt, shorts and shirt as he fled.

Morgan later told me that as a result of this, one of the onlookers, a young homosexual man, after having seen Morgan in his naked glory, never stopped sending him suggestive text messages. This reminded me of the story of my beloved chimp Joseph, who had had free run of my farm in Kenya. Joseph walked into the bathroom one evening as Lee Harrigan, a famous lawyer and great ladies' man, was relieving himself. Joseph crept up behind him and grabbed hold of his manhood. This was during one of Mummy's parties on the farm and I heard Joseph's hoots of delight coming from down the passage accompanied by a man shouting, 'Oh my God, oh my God'. I rushed to see what was happening and there was Lee dancing about shouting with Joseph clinging on for dear life and hooting with delight.

I said to Lee, 'Don't take it away; whatever you do, do not take it away!' I could see myself being sued for loss of a male member! I ran and got a bottle of whisky, since Joseph like all primates loved alcohol, and I gradually managed to coax him into exchanging the bottle for Lee's manhood. Lee had to go to the doctor the next day as it was so swollen and had fingernail marks all over it. My wonderful Dr Boyle said, 'This was indeed a passionate woman, who is she?' Lee said it was unfortunately not a woman but that crazy girl Patricia de Sales' bloody chimpanzee! (I was Countess de Roussy de Sales at that time as I was still married to Aymon). Many years later when I was teasing Lee about all his wives and girlfriends, he said, 'Let's not forget the one homosexual experience in my life which was with your f***ing chimp!'

Another time, we were lunching here with great friends of mine, the Snaiths. Chris had been one of South Africa's top trainers and his wife Sue had always helped him with the stable management, being a very good horsewoman herself. Chris has now retired and his sons have taken over and become just as well known and respected as their father. On this day they had a lady client from England with them. Kalu somehow escaped from her enclosure and next thing appeared at the lunch table. With her penchant for beautiful men she headed straight towards the blond beauty which was Chris Snaith. She sat on his lap, and then, luckily to Chris's delight and not horror, started hugging and kissing him and drinking all the wine in his glass. Then she seized the bottle which she spied in the middle of the table and made short work of that. Looking around for more, she suddenly noticed all the bracelets on the English lady's arm. She climbed down off the table and went over to inspect this new arm covered in bracelets – she is so used to mine, which I have worn since the days of my beloved Tana. Tana used to like walking with my arm in her mouth, so I used to wear all these bracelets, as no matter how gentle she was, sometimes her huge teeth would leave pink marks and the bracelets stopped this from happening. Now Kalu goes up to our guest and taking her arm proceeds to examine her bracelets one by one. Afterwards this lady remarked that the closest she had ever been to a wild animal before this occasion was a squirrel in Hyde Park in London. I thought she had been remarkably composed, given this information!

Sue Snaith is also very blond and beautiful, and in addition a very good horsewoman. Years ago she used to lead the parade into the ring and down to the start on major race days. Recently they came to see me, armed as usual with wonderful gifts, and Sue told me a lovely story about her latest acquisition. A couple of weeks earlier, she found a tiny white dove lying half-dead in her garden. She rushed it to the vet, who gave it an injection of Baytril and showed her how to inject the dove, if by any chance it survived the night. Sue bought it a cage and a child's hot water bottle in the shape of a teddy bear. Not only was it very sick, but highly traumatised too. The next morning, she found it inside the teddy bear, curled up with the hot water bottle. Sue nursed it back to health and found out that it was a Java dove, otherwise known as a sacred white dove, the ones used by magicians as they are so small and become very tame.

Sue decided that now the dove was well it was only fair to put it outside so that it could find its own way home. Chris came in a few hours later and said, 'Your dove is still sitting on the hedge; I don't think it has any intention of finding its way home.' Sue went outside and it immediately flew onto her shoulder. Ever since then it has been her constant companion and follows her everywhere.

Chris then told of how he recently came home to find Sue sobbing her heart out. 'What is the matter, what on earth has happened?' he asked. Through the sobs, Sue told him she could not find her dove and was terrified that either the dogs or the cats had eaten him. Chris searched around and finally spotted the little thing sitting on top of the ceiling light where it was obviously nice and warm. The lampshade was white so the bird had been barely visible. Sue is now back with her constant companion, and rather like I once was with my beloved Molly, her dove travels everywhere with her and the dogs.

Chris Snaith has some wonderful racing stories, one of which is a classic. When he first started training money was still thin on the ground, so when he went to an auction after the races he was tempted by a yearling going for R500 whose name was Corcovado. Chris's clients, Malherbe, Kirkman and Curry, bought him and Chris took him home and put him out into the paddock with the other yearlings.

When Corcovado went into training he never showed much, so he was turned out in the paddock again and more or less forgotten about. Chris then spoke to the owners and suggested they try and sell him for the same R500 they had paid for him, but nobody in the racing world was interested. Eventually they managed to sell him to a lady who owned a riding school. Not long after she bought him she too decided to recoup her R500 and a vet was sent out to give the horse a clean bill of health before the new owners bought it. The vet said he was failing the horse on three counts – heart murmurs, bad joints and a suspect tendon. Chris was forced to refund her the R500 and take the horse back. Once more out into the paddock he went. Some months later an African gentleman arrived looking for a riding horse and he happily bought Corcovado for R500. The next day the new owner arrived with a Volkswagen panel van – a vehicle that could never carry a horse and particularly such a large one. Chris however was determined to get rid of Corcovado and was thinking how to make the horse fit when Sue came along and threatened to report both of them to the SPCA if they continued trying to load a horse into a van that was much too small for it.

She made Chris give the man back his money and once more Corcovado was returned to the paddock. During all the time he was in the paddock, Sue had been feeding him racehorse cubes normally reserved for horses in training. Chris finally decided to enter him into a race for the hell of it, took him out of the paddock and put him into training for seven days. Everyone at the races asked what on earth he was doing racing this rather horrible-looking beast who by now had a long coat as he was never stabled and was covered in bites from the other horses, and not groomed to boot!

At the start Corcovado broke loose, galloped up the course, hurdled two gates and landed on the cement. He then slid to the ground and ended up with even more wounds. Back to the paddock he went. Sue nursed him back to health and Chris decided to enter him again in a 1 000 metre maiden race. He also decided to put blinkers on him and instructed his jockey – the famous Garth Puller – to keep him at the back of the field and to be very careful, as he had a heart problem and could die at any moment. 'At the 200 metre mark, if he has not broken down, just see if he can accelerate at all,' was Chris's advice to Garth. At the 200 metres, Garth takes him to the inside rail and asks him for a bit of an effort, being aware that his heart might not be up to it. The bit of extra effort he asked for ended up turning into a three-length win; Corcovado had won in a canter! Everyone except the horse was in a state of collapse. How was it possible for this ugly, unkempt horse, full of battle scars, with just seven days of training from the paddock, to achieve such a miracle?

This was just the beginning of many more miracles. Suffice to say Corcovado did not return to the paddock but went straight home into a proper stable at night and with a bit of pampering, the right food and some serious training, he became the famous Corcovado, winning 12 races – and all this from a measly R500 that nobody wanted to pay for him! He became a racing hero and won them all an absolute fortune.

Chris, by the time I met him, had already become a famous trainer with lots of horses in his stables. I used to love visiting them. They had bought a large farm at Philippi, which they turned into their training establishment, with their own house, stables and tracks. Gradually the area around the Philippi Training Stables got more and more built up and it was around this time that an owner-trainer called Heather Simpson came to live nearby with a few of her horses. One morning, after she had returned from working the horses, a van drove into the stable yard and when Heather went up to see what the occupants wanted, they shot her twice and then drove off. Thank heavens, she had asked the jockey who had been riding work with her to come and have a cup of tea. When he turned up 10 minutes later she was lying on the ground and asked him to help her up, as she had no feeling in her legs. If he had not come along she would probably have died. As a result of the shooting she was paralysed from the waist down. Nothing had been stolen, although she had the week's wages in her car.

Not long after this, the Snaiths had all their saddles and bridles stolen, so they decided to build a security fence around their property and at the entrance gates put a large electronic screen, so they could monitor everyone going in or out. In addition to this, they decided to buy two ostriches from up-country, as they are known to make marvellous guards. I had a friend in Kenya who did the same thing. Ostriches were not very well known in the area at that time; they are huge birds and have a lethal kick but they can also become very tame and affectionate; the one in Kenya used to follow me around begging for the sweets he knew were always in my pockets.

Not long after they had all this extra security installed along with the two ostriches, the alarm went off. Sue went rushing over to the monitor and there were six strange African gentlemen peering through the glass screen. Sue watched as the ostriches, upon hearing the alarm, approached the gate as they had been taught to do. Soon the ostriches and the strange men were eyeballing each other in the glass screen, at which stage Sue shouted loudly through the intercom system, 'What are you doing here?' One man fell over backwards in terror and the others took flight. They obviously thought they were about to be attacked by these huge speaking monsters from another planet.

CHAPTER

18

I have never been much of a shopper; even with clothes I battle to find much enthusiasm. I used to refuse fittings at Dior and the like and so my poor mother used to buy me the end-of-year collection. As I was very slim, this suited me fine, but being on the farm all day with all the animals meant that these outfits were only ever worn on special occasions, while the more useful practical clothes were worn year after year. Nowadays, since I have so often just got out of a car where I have had a baby baboon clutching its bottle on my shoulder and several slobbering dogs in the back seat I often look like anything but the lady of the manor.

As my friends the Becks owned Stuttafords, I shopped there often. On one occasion I had been to the pet shop inside the store, where there were a lot of birds hopping about within the confines of their cages. Thinking to myself that they would probably remain in small cages for the rest of their lives no matter who bought them, and as money was no object in those days, I decided to buy the lot. There was a charming Indian man in charge of the pet department and I asked him if he could keep them all until I had built suitable aviaries. I assured him I would pay for their upkeep in the meantime, so this was then agreed upon and I paid for the lot – the sum of which was rather large to say the least!

The next day, on my way to the Milnerton racecourse to gallop the horses, I passed a shop that had an extra-large television set displayed in the window. I had not seen anything like it before, so I decided that after the gallops I would go and investigate. It was still early morning, shortly after the gallops at Milnerton, when I parked my old Mercedes – which was as always full of dogs and a few baboons – outside the shop. When I walked in the door the assistant was on the phone and paid no attention to me. Between calls I managed to tell him that I was interested in the big television set in the window. He looked at me, looked at the window and then looked utterly shocked. It was far too expensive for me, he said; they had some smaller second-hand sets at the back that I might be interested in? He beckoned an assistant and went back to his calls.

The assistant obviously also thought I was some poor tramp of a female as I was still dressed in my work clothes. I finally lost patience and informed him that I wanted to buy the television no matter what the cost was, so would he please inform his boss? I could see them looking at me with great suspicion; the assistant came back to say they would need a reference from the bank. The banks opened at 9am and it was only 8.30am. I was not prepared to wait another half an hour, but I suddenly had a brainwave: 'You can call up the gentleman in charge of the pet department at Stuttafords,' I said. 'He knows me well and I bought a lot of birds from him yesterday.' They finally condescended to call Stuttafords, where the person on the phone informed them that I was a great friend of the Becks and a very well-known Stuttaford's customer and had spent a fortune on buying all their birds just yesterday. I don't know what else was said, but the difference in their attitude was nothing short of unbelievable. Of course I could have the television! They could not do enough for me. The result was that I came away with what was then the largest and latest model of television.

Another instance where my poor dressing habits came into play was with Mercedes-Benz in Cape Town. Since my rally driving days I have always been passionate about cars, and never get rid of one that has been good to me. After my beloved Citroën got smashed up by a friend I had lent it to in Kenya, I bought a Mercedes, as the owner of Mercedes-Benz in Kenya, Rex Dobie, was a great friend of mine. On the dirt roads it was not nearly as good as the Citroën, as it was not a front-wheel-drive, but it was great on the tarmac roads. It was the car I brought to South Africa and after I married Frank I took it twice to Australia, where I drove it around at vast speeds. Back in South Africa, I drove it everywhere – to Durban, Johannesburg and beyond. It was bright green and it always pleased me when I sailed past some gentleman who would be furious at having a woman driver pass him. It is indeed amazing how annoyed some men can get!

In the sixties in Kenya, as with so many other things, driving was a relaxed affair and I loved flying along at 120mph with clouds of dust in my wake. Stan banned me from driving anything but the International in his presence, but my family – and my animals – would sleep soundly as we hurtled along. There was a taste of things to come one day, however, as I rounded a corner on the Langata road between Karen and Nairobi and two white speed cops flagged me down. I drew into the side and, as they walked to the car, I thought that once they saw its occupants, I'd probably be let off. They looked inside and couldn't have missed Tana, who was occupying the entire back seat, and a chimpanzee standing on his head in the front seat. To my amazement and with total sangfroid, they wrote out a speeding ticket and never a comment was passed. I was most put out by their indifference but amused to think how coolly they had played it. I wonder if they ever dined out on the story of the day they ticketed a speeding lioness?

I made the big mistake of lending my Mercedes to Frank, who has never been a good driver, and of course he went and had an accident. Not wanting to get rid of the car, I retired it to our big barn. Now I had to get a new one, so I went to Mercedes in Somerset West, where they knew me well, and I made the purchase. A few months later, while driving to Cape Town with Shelagh, an electrical fault brought the car to a standstill. This was certainly not the best area for two women on their own to be, but amazingly, two gentlemen in a Mercedes going in the opposite direction, seeing our problem, turned around and stayed with us until Mercedes Somerset West sent a car out to rescue us.

A few days later I decided to go to Cape Town to see what latest models they had displayed in their showroom. There was a magnificent 500 model that had just arrived. The engine was so powerful – double the power of a normal one – I knew I had to have it.

Back in the seventies, women in this country were often regarded as second-class citizens and car salesmen were certainly not used to a woman coming in and buying her own luxury vehicle, and certainly not one dressed in rather grubby old clothing the way I was dressed that day. More or less the same thing happened; I was fobbed off once more with second-hand models, much resistance and many questions as to where my husband might be. Realising that I was getting nowhere I knew I would have to resort to making a phone call, so I told the salesman that I was definitely taking the 500 and he was to call up the manager of Mercedes-Benz in Somerset West and tell him the Hon Mrs P O'Neill of Broadlands Stud Farm is here to buy their 500. Once again the same scenario ensued and the manager rushed out with the salesman to tell me I could buy their entire fleet if that was my wish. They then insisted that the 500 be brought out for me to test drive. I was delighted with its acceleration and it became another treasured car.

Ten years ago, I found out about a man who was stealing money off John, an old-age pensioner who used to work for me on the farm. This man used to drive John to pick up his pension every month, then keep the money and give John a basic amount. I could not understand why old John was having a problem every month finding enough food to feed himself. This had apparently been going on for several years. I reported the man to the police, with the result that one night, supposedly as an act of revenge, he came and set fire to the vehicles in the garage. Up in smoke went my beautiful Mercedes, along with Frank's Mercedes, Shelagh's Honda Civic and the farm's work bakkie. What a senseless waste! With the insurance money I bought the same model, but this time around it had to be a second-hand version as I no longer have the money to buy top-of-the-range motor cars.

So once again I have a precious car, but these days I do feel I am taking my life in my hands when I drive! In my opinion the utter lack of concentration given to the act of driving these days results in so many accidents. Drivers talk to passengers, chat on their cell-phones and fiddle with their music systems – they almost never hold the steering wheel correctly, which in my mind is criminal as the slightest thing happens and they cannot then control the car. As for rearview mirrors and side mirrors – well, they might as well not exist, along with red lights – the other day I could not believe it, I counted six cars pass by me on a red light. Admittedly, there was nothing coming on the side roads, but a red light is a red light!

* * *

Every year we get so many interesting guests coming to stay, mostly great friends of my brother's. Last year we had a very glamorous lady called Margaret Spittle staying with us. Her married name is Hare but she has kept her maiden name, as she has made it so famous. Margaret is one of the world's leading oncologists. All her life, even as a child, her one ambition was to become a doctor. When she was in her teens, being very good looking, it was suggested she became an actress and she got a place at the Royal Academy of the Dramatic Arts (RADA). As she laughingly told us, 'The two professions are after all very similar.' Her flirtation with acting was short-lived as she persuaded her parents to let her go to Westminster Hospital Medical School, where she discovered that her burning ambition in life was to concentrate on cancer research, combining the technical aspect of radiation with the medical aspect of chemotherapy and the psychological aspect of coping with a life-threatening disease.

Margaret was given the great honour of being awarded an OBE by Her Majesty the Queen for her services to medicine. Recently, she was appointed as civilian adviser in radiation medicine to the Royal Navy, so on occasion she has to inspect nuclear submarines, as well as being a member of the Nuclear Defence Safety

Committee. It was while she was chairing a committee on the malevolent use of radiation that the most extraordinary coincidence occurred. The world had just discovered that a radioactive substance had been used to poison Alexander Litvinenko, a Russian who was once a member of the KGB. He was a man who held many national secrets, and the Russians were afraid of what he might tell the English. An agent was therefore sent over to kill him by administering radioactive polonium in his tea at the Grosvenor Hotel in London. Apparently the dose given was so potent it could have killed 40 people. This was the first poisoning of its kind and in spite of all Margaret's knowledge there was nothing that could be done to save him.

Considerable radioactivity was detected in London where the Russians had stayed and on the aircrafts they had flown in, but there was amazingly little panic amongst the population – possibly, it was suggested, because the incident coincided with the release of the latest James Bond film.

Margaret, in spite of her incredible lifestyle, is such a lovely, unassuming woman. She also became the first female committee member of the Air Squadron, of which my brother Caryll Waterpark was a founder when he was head of CSE Aviation. She still flies her old twin-engine Aztec as a hobby, and in spite of her enduring relationship with my brother, she is continually offended when he refers to her beloved aircraft as 'a bag of flying rivets'.

Another guest, John Scurr, is a surgeon with a special interest in vascular surgery. Over the years he had treated a lot of patients with deep vein thrombosis, but then, in one short period, he had to treat a pop star, an airline president and a member of the House of Lords, all of whom had recently been on a long-distance flight. Looking through his records, he found that a lot of his previous patients with blood clots had been flying – and thus the link was made. Being a very famous surgeon and a pilot, he approached one of the airlines and asked them to assist with his research – which resulted in many plane-loads of people half of whom were wearing elastic compression stockings! He soon discovered that there was a much higher incidence of deep vein thrombosis in those not wearing the compression stockings.

John then got a group of doctors with similar interests together under the auspices of the World Health Organisation. The resulting WRIGHT project – World Health Organisation Research Into Global Hazards of Travel – commemorated the hundredth anniversary of the Wright brothers' first flight and resulted in the drug Zinopin, which stops people getting blood clots while flying. Aspirin is the alternative, but it disagrees with a lot of people – though, interestingly, John says that approximately 50 tons of aspirin are carried up and down Oxford Street in women's handbags every day!

John, with his great looks and enormous success has, much like my great friend Chris Barnard, been a bit of a magnet to adoring staff and women. John has been married twice and now has a lovely partner, the Hon Persephone Brigstocke, who is the mother of his beautiful five-year-old twins. He has eight children in total, three from his first wife, three from his second and then the twins. Two sons are doctors, one a surgeon and one a paediatrician; another is a medical student. The other three are a Cambridge don, a historical biographer, and an airline pilot.

Persephone is a great animal lover and part of my animal trust. She has had a very interesting life. During the last world war, when she was still a child, she lived in Washington DC, as her father was in the British Embassy. Her mother persuaded Jacqueline Kennedy to accept Persephone as the only foreign child in the nursery school that was run at the White House. Her best friend at the time was

Caroline Kennedy, who would often come to visit her and was always accompanied by her two bodyguards. Persephone's mother was an expert on education and Greek classical history, hence Persephone's name. She used to read poems and stories of those times to the two girls. The bodyguards were soon sound asleep with boredom, and one of them used to snore gently, forcing her mother to raise her voice to enable the girls to hear these classical tales.

When Persephone was 16 and living back in England, she was doing her homework one evening when her father called from Orly Airport in Paris and said, 'Tell your mother not to come to the airport, as I am going to be late – Air France has gone on strike, so I will be coming on Turkish Airlines.' Persephone had the television on and was still doing her homework, when news came through of a Turkish Airline crash – at the time the largest crash in aviation history. She finally got through on a help line to be told that there were no survivors. Her mother called up a little while later and said, 'Let me speak to your father, he must be home by now,' and Persephone had to tell her the terrible news, although she knew it would ruin her mother's life. Her mother had just accepted the job of High Mistress of St Paul's Girls School. Years later, in 1996, she was given a political peerage and the title of baroness by the Queen due to her work in education. Sadly, in 2004, while in Greece attending a conference, she and a colleague left the venue to go across the street to the hotel in which they were staying. They crossed the road at a pedestrian crossing and were waiting in the middle before proceeding to the other side, when the drivers of speeding cars racing each other saw them; the first managed to avoid them but the second did not have time to swerve, and killed them both.

Persephone and John met on a night out with friends. She was a very glamorous casualty nurse at the time. He needed a qualified person to run his practice and offered her the job. She became his personal assistant and learned to fly his helicopter and his jet. They now have a farm in Wiltshire, as Persephone wanted to assist in saving Asian moon bears from farms where they spend their lives in agony in a cage with a permanent tube inserted into their bile ducts to drain the bile. This traditional medicine supposedly cures a range of ailments. It is truly horrific!

Today Persephone is involved in rescuing battery hens for the British Hen Welfare Trust. Once the commercial laying life of a hen is over and they are of no further use to the farmer, they are released to the Trust – and as a result Persephone now has lots of hens! She tells me that when they first arrive, they are traumatised and cannot walk as many of them have broken legs. They are featherless and terrified. Within a matter of weeks, with veterinary treatment, proper food and tender, loving care their feathers start coming back, their leg muscles build up strength again and at mealtimes they all crowd around her. She purchased a large cockerel that she named Neville. He is a complete gentleman, looks after the hens, summons them for food at meal times, and waits until they have eaten before taking his own food. He sidles up to them to show his affection for whichever hen has taken his fancy. Mostly it is Persephone herself, whom he adores. He sits on her lap while she is watching television and follows her around the house. Persephone laughingly complains that he thinks he is in charge of the house as well.

CHAPTER

19

Not all our visitors to Broadlands come from far afield; a regular visitor is one of my great friends, Elizabeth Wilson, who I met years ago through racing. She and her husband, Robin, were a very good-looking pair: she very glamorous, with a lovely figure; he with fair hair to complement her brunette locks. He was also a famous polo player at the time and quite a catch. I have always loved the story of how Elizabeth persuaded Robin to propose. They were very young and had been dating for some time, but he never 'popped the important question'. One evening they were invited to a fancy-dress ball, so Elizabeth decided to make a statement in front of all their friends and dressed herself up as a bride. She wore a beautiful wedding dress complete with flowers and with one of her friends as a bridesmaid. It worked and today, 52 years later, they are still married, with a lovely daughter and grandchildren. Although I often tell her I have no idea how Robin has put up with her for so long.

Elizabeth's daughter was married here at Broadlands. The wedding was enormous, with marquees and a flood of champagne for the hundreds of guests. Thousands of white roses lined the walkway to the reception as the lovely bride and her new husband arrived – it was terribly glamorous!

Elizabeth was once the editor of South Africa's *Racehorse* magazine, which became *SA Horseman*, and used to write an introductory column which was often very scathing of various people in racing news. I nicknamed her 'the poison pen' and looked forward to reading this monthly piece of 'news'. She has been a wonderful friend to me over the years, but I cannot get her to give up smoking, even though at one stage her heart collapsed and she had to be rushed to Casualty. I keep telling her that if I could give up, so bloody well could she, but of course she pays me absolutely no attention – a typical trait in smokers!

* * *

A beloved yearly visitor is my dear husband Frank. Today, because Frank gets his pension and free medical assistance in Australia, he spends nine months of the year there and comes to stay with me at Broadlands for the other three months. My brother usually has lots of guests from England during the summer months, and Frank, because of all his swimming, does not hear too well. Deafness runs in his family and he feels embarrassed having to socialise with a lot of strangers, so he asked if I could give him a little apartment of his own. A few years ago I built him a small one-bedroom apartment and put a nice big double bed in there, but the room is not very big, so when he called up and asked if he could bring his lady friend with him, as she was so marvellous to him and let him share her flat at Manly, I had to find out if they shared a bed. I needed to know if I should buy another bed and put this in the little open-plan sitting room. I finally spoke to her on the telephone when Frank called up to tell me their arrival time. I gathered up my courage to ask her about their sleeping arrangements and learned that a double bed was fine. She sounded charming and asked me if I did not mind. I told her I was delighted that he had someone who was so good to him and looked after him so well. I am looking forward to seeing them both again this year.

This brings to mind another story. Years ago, I got a call from an island off Australia. The operator put me through and it was Frank on the line. 'Darling,' he said, 'you have got to get me out of here. I am with a very passionate lady but her husband is also here. Early in the morning, as soon as he goes out fishing, she climbs into my bed. I think he is beginning to suspect something. I am finding it very difficult to concentrate; I am sure he is going to come back early and surprise us one day. He has not got the best of reputations and will as sure as hell put the heavies onto me. Send me a telegram that I am urgently needed on the farm and you want me to fly home.'

A few minutes later I got a call from the operator. 'Are you really Mrs O'Neill, the wife of Swimmer O'Neill?' he asked. I said, 'Yes, and I have just been talking to my husband.' The operator confessed, 'I have always been a fan of his so I listened in to your conversation. I cannot believe what I heard. Do you really not mind your husband having an affair with another woman? On top of which he is asking you to rescue him from his own folly. Don't you hate him for what he is doing to you?'

Feeling very much like my mother I said, 'Of course not. He is a lovely person. As well as my husband, he is my best friend. I will do whatever I can for him.'

'Well,' he said, 'I have heard everything now!'

I have often thought of that operator on some semi-deserted atoll. How stunned he must have been.

* * *

After the publication of *A Lion in the Bedroom* I met up with the most wonderful and fascinating man, John Rendall, who wrote a book called *A Lion called Christian*. John came to visit me here at Broadlands not very long ago and we stay in regular contact. He and a friend, Ace Bourke, went over to England as young students from Australia in the sixties. One day in the pet department in Harrods they found a lion cub and after much debate they bought him and took him back to their flat in Chelsea. What follows is the most wonderful story of their relationship with their beloved lion, Christian. I have read the book twice now and it reduces me to tears as it brings back so many wonderful memories of my precious Tana. Eventually John and Ace flew Christian to Kenya and stayed with George Adamson at Kora, so that George could eventually introduce Christian to the wild. Much later John Rendall read my book and came to see me when he was in South Africa. The love he shared with Christian is now seen so often on television as well as on You Tube, where the film clip of Christian and John reuniting went viral. He and Ace had gone to Kora to see Christian who had his own pride. The wonderful sight of this huge male lion leaving his pride and racing up to them and nearly bowling them over with his love is astonishingly beautiful. It is true a lion never forgets. John is now a Trustee of the George Adamson Trust which administers the Mkomazi National Park in Tanzania and Kora National Park where Christian was reintroduced to the wild – this was the Park adjoining Meru where my beautiful Tana was released in 1964.

John also takes safaris out to Kenya once a year. As well as taking people to Kora he also takes them to Meru and shows them where I lived with Tana. My beautiful lodge that I built on the banks of the Rojewero River does not exist any more, only the foundations are there. He tells me that there are still remnants of the 3 000 pawpaw trees which I had planted for my precious herd of elephants. It is so wonderful to think that John Rendall due to his love of lions still spends his life involved with these wonderful animals.

* * *

A wonderful story about Jim Antrobus, our beloved vet from so many years ago, dates from the 2012 yearling sales in Cape Town. Jim had a very well-bred colt on the sale, by Dynasty out of Something of Value. The dam of Something of Value was a horse I had given to Jim years ago. She was Masai Mara, named after one of my favourite places in Kenya, where I once had a tented camp teeming with game of all descriptions. When I gave her to Jim I promised him he could take her once she went to stud. While we weren't expecting great things from her, she went and surprised us and won seven races. Jim felt he could no longer accept her as a gift as she was now far too valuable, but I was furious and so he agreed to take her and thanked me for the gift, but then told me he would give her back to me as a gift! I was having none of this and told him that Masai Mara was his and that was that. John Freeman, Jim remembers, was livid with me for giving her away, but I really wanted Jim to have her. When her foal was born, Jim named her Something of Value after the book written by Robert Ruark on the Mau Mau uprising by Kenyan rebels against British rule. It was wonderful that Jim kept up the Kenyan link with this name.

So there Jim was, many years later, hoping to earn a little money from the colt that had come from my gift. This colt turned out to be a magnificent-looking yearling: with the advice of Mike Sharkey, a stud manager of the Becks at Highlands stud farm, Jim decided that his true value would be R150 000 and had therefore put this reserve on him. He was very worried that they had overestimated his price and that he would not reach the reserve, especially since this was a local Cape Town sale and not the big Easter Sale in Johannesburg. If this happened, they would have to resort to selling the colt privately for whatever they could get. On the sale day Jim, his wife Merle and two daughters were all at the ringside to watch their colt come into the ring. Mike had assured Jim that there had been a lot of interest on the farm from various trainers and agents and that David Nagel, one of the big stud owners in Ireland, had remarked that the colt was an outstanding walker (this being of utmost importance in a good racehorse).

The auctioneers at a horse sale usually start with the reserve and then go down the scale to get the first bid, which was R50 000. Panicking, Jim feared the worst, but the bidding continued – and then, much to his delight, gathered speed. It was with a feeling of euphoria that he watched the R150 000 come up on the screen, and from there it just took off. At R200 000 Merle was so excited, she said to Jim. 'You're making so much money, I want a boob job!' Bidding did not stop there and the Antrobus family were astounded when it climbed to over a million. The two daughters now added to Jim's shopping list, asking for a new horse and a few new saddles and bridles.

At one and a half million a hush had descended and the Antrobus family were all clutching hands in a state of shock: never in their wildest dreams had they imagined being able to make this kind of money. The colt sold for two and a half million and the entire family was in floods of tears. This magnificent colt had secured their future, as Jim had been worried about when he would have to retire and how he would be able to keep his farm going. This gift from God transformed his life and that of his family and I can honestly say that no man deserves such a gift more than Jim, who dedicated his life to animals and worked so selflessly, in spite of his back problems, on all my animals, from Kalu through to my jackals, caracals, macaws and more.

CHAPTER

20

While life today at Broadlands is very different, I still live surrounded by my animals. I think people would be amazed to see this old lady of 87's sleeping arrangements, but at least I do not now have the chimpanzee and the baboons to add to my night-time woes. I have six dogs on the bed at night, and two cats. Two of the dogs are Great Danes, my beloved Nguni and Madubi. Nguni is such a mother's boy, he has to sleep with his head on the pillow next to mine. He will not even eat his food unless I am sitting next to him and then I have to look at him and say 'eat'. At night, just to make my life more comfortable, he often has dreams; his tail thumps away against the bed, his legs twitch and the whole bed starts to shake. They are obviously happy dreams, but in order to get some sleep I wake him gently by kissing and patting his head. Madubi is also a great dreamer, but not nearly as energetic as her brother. Honey Bunch, the 'bloody cat' insists on sleeping under the blanket, with her head next to my face. Then a paw comes out, at least four times a night, which means she is hungry and expects me to get up and feed her. She can only eat small quantities at a time, otherwise she gets sick, so I have to wake up, climb out of bed and feed her. She is so spoilt; she will only eat a certain tin of cat food, which has to be the most expensive, of course! In addition to this, she refuses to eat anything left over in the tin, even though it has been kept in the fridge.

I suppose the other good thing to come out of being woken up through the night, is that it gives me a chance to feed all the feral cats. They come through the old baboon cage to my bathroom, 12 of them, and they consume vast quantities of tinned cat food, biscuits, chicken and milk. The bowls have to be constantly replenished. One of them is the most glorious of animals and adores me. He purrs loudly as soon as he sees me and has become unbelievably affectionate, even insisting on sitting on my lap when I am on the toilet. The others will all come inside but as soon as I make any movement, they take off. I have only managed to get half of them neutered, and must somehow find a way of trapping the others before spring comes.

While carnivores and primates make up the majority of animals at Broadlands, some much-loved goats also deserve a mention. Billy, the beloved Broadlands goat, arrived on the scene when a herdboy was trespassing on the farm, grazing his goats. One of his old nanny goats died giving birth to twins, one of which survived, and Shelagh, hearing of the birth, rushed down to rescue the kid before it met an untimely end. Billy was brought up to the house and, naturally, raised in her bed with all her dogs and cats. I had to buy special milk for him, only the best and most expensive, and when he got too old for his nappies, Shelagh put him into a playpen at night with pillows and blankets. During the day Billy followed Shelagh everywhere, surrounded by her accompanying troop of dogs, but at night he still insisted on sleeping on her bed. Overseas guests arriving for the summer months would occasionally come across a spray of goat droppings in the corridors, something I knew would not go down too well with the English contingent, so as Billy was now nine months old it was decided to put him in Kalu's old camp. We bought him a female companion whom Shelagh named Belinda. She is a white goat with golden ears, while Billy has a magnificent golden brown coat that shines brilliantly in the sunshine.

Billy, being Billy, had to have a shed built for his night-time use and I was then sent off to buy a bed, which of course had to have a mattress, a cover and pillows, because they all had to be washed and kept clean. As if this was not enough, I was then sent off to buy tables because by this time it was established that Billy, like most goats, did not like sleeping on the ground. With winter round the corner, spoilt Billy and his companion have had to move to new quarters because he does not like getting his feet wet and insists on remaining inside when it rains, so Shelagh, poor woman, has to walk through the puddles twice a day to give him his feed. These beloved goats enjoy Marie biscuits and oats and I must say it is wonderful to see them lying in the sun on their tables while they wait for Shelagh to come down in the late afternoon and pamper them. Billy still enjoys an hour's walk a day with his friends the dogs and his beloved Shelagh when she goes to inspect her horses.

A number of other goats live with Kalu in her enclosure. The other day I had just spread their usual evening treat of carrots, apples and bread all over the concrete slab which was built for this purpose outside Kalu's bedroom door, as putting food on the grass was not practical from a cleanliness point of view. Sitting on my bench outside the bedroom door, I waited for Kalu's arrival.

Kalu had been sitting in her second camp at the top of a giant fir tree. Here she has made a huge nest for herself from where she can survey the world. The agility with which this huge ape climbs up and down is truly amazing. Sliding down her tree when she saw me, she came striding towards me where I sat surrounded by goats. She shoved them aside with her hand and then seized the very old goat that often follows her around by the hind leg. I was surprised that the goat did not seem to mind, and was just about to go to her rescue when Kalu let go of the leg and grabbed her by one of her horns. The goat still showed no signs of worry – then, to my amazement, Kalu started stroking her with her other hand and patting her under her chin. The goat had her head in Kalu's lap and was loving all this attention. Once she had finished stroking the goat, Kalu started picking up the carrots from the floor and trying to feed her. The goat sadly was not interested in being hand fed. My worry is that this little old goat is not much longer for this world – in spite of all the grass and food, she is not in good condition – and that when she departs this world, Kalu will go into another stage of mourning like she did when her beloved Piggy died and she forced me to walk through the muddy field so that she could show me his dead body, then refused to eat for days.

* * *

In the foothills of the Helderberg Mountains, just up the road, we have built an Animal Care Facility on the outskirts of Sir Lowry's Village. The seven million that I got for the farm when I sold it was put into an Animal Trust and used to buy the land and build the enclosures and accommodation for Morgan and some staff, but almost all of this has now been spent. My younger brother kindly loaned me R700 000 to get water laid out to all the enclosures, for the electrified fencing and to build a firebreak around the entire area. It is not far from Broadlands and the primates enjoy an uninterrupted view down to the azure seas below. Morgan has designed the most beautiful enclosures with tree houses, ropes, rocks and enormous branches for the primates to enjoy.

Each baboon enclosure has its own room built on the ground, with of course a large shelf for them to sleep on at night time, with a ladder up to it. George, one of the older baboons, has chosen one particular tree for his daily ritual of clambering up to sit on a branch and watch the sun set over the bay below. My beloved Bingo does the same, but since he is such an old gentleman, Morgan has built him a platform in the tree, so that he does not have to balance on a branch to watch the sun sink below the horizon. Little Elgin, the youngest member of the clan, has also been spoilt: Morgan has built him a swimming pool, which was quite an expense! It is made out of natural rocks and on hot days Morgan goes into the pool with him, as he says, to keep him company.

We have moved all the primates there, except Kalu – and what an exercise this was, as they all needed to be darted and moved quickly before they woke. The end result of all of our efforts has been amazing and Morgan along with his 11 dogs and various cats as well as all the baboons and vervets are most happy in their new home. At the moment Kalu sleeps next to her keeper Michael and his wife, with a window off her sleeping platform into their bedroom. From here she can watch television and listen to their music and conversation. I cannot imagine what other things she must see and hear! She is madly in love with Michael and gets quite frantic if he ever goes away for a night.

* * *

In 2011, I had to sell what was left of my jewellery and when Antony Beck and his mother, Rhona, heard about this they called up Elresia Myburgh, a trustee of the Beck Foundation, to find out what was going on. With all the money that was being spent on the Animal Care Facility I could no longer draw on the trust money for personal expenses. Once again my beloved friend Shelia Southey came to my rescue and bought my engagement ring, a Cartier diamond and gold ring that Mummy had bought for me all those years ago when I had married Frank for the first time. She then gave it back to me! Not long after this Elresia came to see me. She told me that Rhona and Antony were so worried about my lack of finances that they were going to give me a monthly income. How absolutely wonderful to have such incredible friends!

I am so grateful to Chris Myburgher – what a wonderful friend he has turned out to be! The trustees of my Animal Trust had been advised by their financial adviser to invest the money with Relative Value Arbitrage Fund, a hedge fund which was making about 20 per cent return on the money invested with it. In July 2012 the two directors had a fight in their office. One shot and killed his partner and then shot and killed himself. Billions had been lost in what is now shown to have been a Ponzi scheme and some people have lost all their life savings. My trustees of course resigned with immediate effect, as all my money had now been lost. Being a brilliant businessman, Chris rushed over and at his own expense has taken over the running of the trust until the disaster has been sorted out. He has even given me the money for the trust wages. I am so blessed to have friends like Antony and Rhona Beck, Chris Myburgher and Sheila Southey! God and my mother have sent them to me and they are in my prayers every night.

* * *

I often think about those most wonderful years of my life, the never-to-be-forgotten times in Kenya, with my beloved lioness Tana. Unfortunately Caryll, my brother, is a neatness fanatic, so unlike my mother and myself, who were and are hoarders par excellence. Many years ago I was out in town and Caryll and Frank decided to take a tour of the attic. They came across tin trunk loads of my old Dior dresses and my many boxes with all my old papers and love letters (I never used to keep diaries, but I did scribble on bits of paper, and many precious memories were stored there). They hauled it all outside and set fire to the lot! I was furious! The other day, by chance, I came across a page. How it escaped the fire I do not know.

The page that survived must have been written at Meru, where I built a lodge on the banks of the Rojewero River, Tana's future home. It reads:

I have just woken up to the wonderful sounds of Africa, my beloved Tana asleep beside me, my arms around her neck, both of us tucked under the mosquito net that hangs from the bedroom ceiling. I am the only white girl in this huge tract of Africa, stretching to the Somaliland border. This beautiful country, the wonderful tribes of Africa and this glorious being, my huge lioness, who is my life.

In the distance I hear the trumpet of an elephant as the herd crosses the river. They will be led by the wonderful old matriarch, whom I have named Mama Mkubwa, meaning Big Mother. They are my beloved herd, I knew them all so well, I often walk with them for miles across the plains and forests, my hand in Mama's mouth. My beloved Africa is on the move, I can hear the cry of the fish eagle. I know that it is time to get up. How blessed I am to have known the incredible love of a lion and to be living such an amazing life in this beautiful country.

Reading that page has been so nostalgic and I have been weeping ever since. Now at the age of 87, I am lying here, still on the beautiful soil of Africa, under the shade of a large pine tree, wrapped in the hairy arms of my beloved chimpanzee, my head on her chest. I can hear her heart beating, the heartbeat of Africa, and the heartbeat of life and of love.

Half asleep, my mind wanders back on my amazing life, thanks to my beloved mother and incredible lioness Tana who gave me the most wonderful years of my life in Kenya and who both taught me the true meaning of love. Now in South Africa, I am also surrounded by love, from my wonderful staff and friends and all my rescued dogs, cats, baboons, vervets – and above all my beautiful, demanding, spoilt and intensely loving Kalu. Thank you, God, for the wonderful gift of life and love you have given me through the years.

RECIPES AND AN EDITOR'S NOTE ON SUNDAY LUNCHES AT BROADLANDS

O ver the years Broadlands has hosted thousands of guests and Pat's potato dishes in particular have become legendary the world over. The first time I visited Pat, her roast potato dish was served at lunch – I have often wondered if this was to ensure that I return for many more lunches while we worked together on this book. Pat is of the belief that many guests come to lunch at Broadlands, not for the company, but for the potato dishes. I am of the belief that people come for both – in equal measures. Over the many Sundays I have spent at Broadlands we have been joined by a number of Pat's friends, each one as entertaining and interesting as the last.

I have, over many months, been fortunate enough to taste the dishes Pat and her staff have shared with her readers below – I will attempt to repeat them in my home and they will forever bring back the taste, sounds and smells of the Broadlands homestead, which despite its decline still dominates the valley below.

Shelagh tells me that as the homestead is protected through heritage laws no development can take place in front of the main home. It is comforting to know that the broad vistas belonging to Broadlands will remain and that future generations may still have a glimpse of a truly historic home where some of the country's greatest racehorses once lived alongside beloved primates, birds, dogs and a host of other wonderful creatures. Today, despite the current financial worries, Pat, Shelagh, Morgan, Amina and Margaret the two cooks, Victoria, Doris and Edna the maids and Hennie and Michael all continue to find a way to care for an enormous number of animals as well as one another, all the while having to contend with unscrupulous opportunists and a great deal of crime – they remain optimistic, up-beat people from whom I have learnt an enormous amount not only about horse racing, baboons, chimps and potatoes, but about honesty, integrity and compassion for things far beyond themselves and this material world.

Donna Cobban

THE RECIPES

Roast Potatoes

Boil potatoes with the skins on, testing with a knife to make sure they are cooked. Then take out and allow to cool. When cold, hand-peel them (not with a knife), as this leaves the potato a bit floury. Cut in half. Have boiling oil ready – I use sunflower oil. Stir fry until golden brown all over, using a spatula to turn them. When light golden brown, take out and put in a dish to cool then salt. Then, 10–15 minutes before eating, have boiling oil ready and put the potatoes in again. Keep stirring until beautifully crisp and flaky. Lightly salt again before serving.

Potato Layer Dish

Boil 2 or 3 large potatoes. Once cooked, line a dish with thin cooked potato slices, then layer with raw onion rings and garlic butter slices as well as salt, pepper and mixed herbs. Continue layering with these ingredients until the dish is almost full. Once you get to the top layer, add half a pot of cream and a tablespoon of cream of chicken soup along with half a mug of boiling water, then top up the dish with milk. To finish off sprinkle a thick layer of cheese on the top. Any cheese can be used, but I prefer a layer of grated Cheddar and a layer of Parmesan. Bake in a 220°C oven for about 15 minutes.

Baked Potato with Cheese Filling

Preheat oven to 220°C. Place 4 large potatoes in centre of oven; remove when cooked and cut into halves. Remove inside of potatoes and put in mixing bowl. Add 1 cup grated Cheddar, ¼ cup Parmesan and ¼ cup garlic butter and mash together. Add salt and pepper to taste. Put filling back into potato shell. Sprinkle some Cheddar cheese on top and put back in oven till brown and crispy.

Roast Chicken

Preheat oven to 220°C. Rub chicken with a little oil and sprinkle with salt and cayenne pepper. Cut 1 apple and 1 onion in pieces and stuff chicken with the apple, onion, rosemary and whatever other mixed herbs you like. Put 2 tablespoons oil in oven pan then add chicken and cook for approx. 2 hours during which time you can every now and then baste the chicken with its own gravy. Chicken must be golden brown with crispy skin when taken out.

Salad Dressing

People are passionate about my salad dressing and there have been innumerable suggestions that I market it, so rather than see it sitting on a supermarket shelf packed with preservatives, I am sharing it here instead:

Take a china bowl about 15 cm high. At the bottom of the bowl, put 4 teaspoons of grated garlic, 2 teaspoons of English mustard, a pinch each of salt and white pepper as well as a generous grind of some coarse black pepper, and a pinch each of cayenne pepper and paprika. Mix well together, then add 750 ml extra virgin olive oil. Mix well with the base, then add 4 tablespoons of apple cider vinegar, 2 tablespoons of Maggi sauce and 2 tablespoons of honey. Whisk all the ingredients together and taste to see if more pepper or salt is needed.